ADMISSION TEST SERIES

ATS-100

D1567365

THIS IS YOUR **PASSBOOK**® FOR ...

CERTIFICATION EXAMINATION FOR HEALTH EDUCATION SPECIALISTS (CHES)

NATIONAL LEARNING CORPORATION®
passbooks.com

Attainment of Certification

Individuals who are certified receive a personalized certificate suitable for framing and may use the abbreviation CHES in listing degrees and other credentials. Also, the NCHEC annually prepares a list of certified health education specialists which is available for a fee, upon request, to professional groups and employing agencies.

Recertification

Recertification is required every five (5) years. Continuing education is required for recertification. Guidelines for recertification are developed by the NCHEC. Failure to pay required fees or to meet continuing education requirements will result in termination of certification. In such cases, it will be necessary to reapply for and to pass the examination in order to become certified again.

THE CERTIFICATION EXAMINATION

The Examination

The examination is practice-based. It tests those aspects of the responsibilities and competencies of entry-level health education specialists that can be measured with a paper-and-pencil examination. The examination, consisting of 150 multiple-choice type questions, is used to measure the possession, application, and interpretation of knowledge essential to the professional practice of health education. Each item has four alternative answers, only one of which is correct. The examination was developed by certified health education specialists working under the direction of PES staff.

The reported score equals the total number of correct responses: there is no penalty for incorrect answers. It is to the candidate's advantage to answer each item even when uncertain of the correct response. The candidate should choose the single best answer to each item. No credit is given for items in which more than one response is selected.

Scope of the Examination

Within each area of responsibility, the major tasks performed by entry-level health education specialists that will be tested have been identified. These task statements serve as the basis for developing the questions on the certification examination. The areas to be included on the examination are:

I. Assess Individual and Community Needs for Health Education
    A. Assess environmental factors (such as social, cultural, political, economic, physical) by gathering health-related data in order to identify health needs.
    B. Assess individual and group characteristics by gathering health related data in order to identify health needs, interests, and concerns.
    C. Assess community and/or individual resources by gathering information in order to determine the feasibility of a health education program.
    D. Interpret assessment and summarize assessment by analyzing environmental, individual and group resource data in order to determine priorities for program development.

II.   Plan Effective Health Education Programs
    A. Collaborate with community agencies and individuals by coordinating resources and services in order to develop an effective health education plan.
    B. Collaborate with potential participants by involving them in the planning process in order to develop a plan acceptable to the participants.
    C. Develop the health education plan to meet health needs by applying theory from such fields as psychology, sociology, education, and biology and integrating the assessment data, community resources and services, and input from potential participants.

III.   Implement the Health Education Program
    A. Implement the health education plan by employing health education methods and techniques in order to achieve program objectives.

IV.   Evaluate Effectiveness of Health Education Program
    A. Develop a program evaluation plan by establishing criteria of effectiveness in order to assess the achievement of program objectives.
    B. Monitor the health education program by reviewing ongoing program activities in order to determine if the program is being implemented as planned.
    C. Monitor the health education program by comparing results with outcome criteria in order to determine program effectiveness.
    D. Modify the health education program as indicated by comparison of results with criteria in order to enhance the likelihood of program success.

V.   Coordinate Provision of Health Education Services
    A. Elicit the cooperation of persons from diverse programs by establishing relationships with and between those individuals in order to coordinate related health education services.

VI.   Act as a Resource Person in Health Education
    A. Select sources of information on health issues by evaluating these sources in order to disseminate health information to individuals and/or groups.
    B. Serve as consultant to individuals and groups by assisting in the identification of issues and recommending alternative strategies in order to meet their needs.

VII.   Communicate Health and Health Education Needs, Concerns, and Resources
    A. Keep abreast of professional literature and current trends and research by reviewing literature and attending professional meetings in order to maintain knowledge and skills.
    B. Advocate for the inclusion of education in health programs and services.
    C. Explain the foundations of the discipline of health education including its purposes, theories, history, ethics, and contributions in order to promote the development and practice of health education.
    D. Select communication methods and techniques by matching characteristics of individual/target group with methods/techniques and issues in order to assess, plan, implement, and evaluate health education services.

HOW TO TAKE A TEST

You have studied long, hard and conscientiously.

With your official admission card in hand, and your heart pounding, you have been admitted to the examination room.

You note that there are several hundred other applicants in the examination room waiting to take the same test.

They all appear to be equally well prepared.

You know that nothing but your best effort will suffice. The "moment of truth" is at hand: you now have to demonstrate objectively, in writing, your knowledge of content and your understanding of subject matter.

You are fighting the most important battle of your life—to pass and/or score high on an examination which will determine your career and provide the economic basis for your livelihood.

What extra, special things should you know and should you do in taking the examination?

I. YOU MUST PASS AN EXAMINATION

A. *WHAT EVERY CANDIDATE SHOULD KNOW*
Examination applicants often ask us for help in preparing for the written test. What can I study in advance? What kinds of questions will be asked? How will the test be given? How will the papers be graded?

B. *HOW ARE EXAMS DEVELOPED?*
Examinations are carefully written by trained technicians who are specialists in the field known as "psychological measurement," in consultation with recognized authorities in the field of work that the test will cover. These experts recommend the subject matter areas or skills to be tested; only those knowledges or skills important to your success on the job are included. The most reliable books and source materials available are used as references. Together, the experts and technicians judge the difficulty level of the questions.

Test technicians know how to phrase questions so that the problem is clearly stated. Their ethics do not permit "trick" or "catch" questions. Questions may have been tried out on sample groups, or subjected to statistical analysis, to determine their usefulness.

Written tests are often used in combination with performance tests, ratings of training and experience, and oral interviews. All of these measures combine to form the best-known means of finding the right person for the right job.

II. HOW TO PASS THE WRITTEN TEST

A. BASIC STEPS

1) Study the announcement

How, then, can you know what subjects to study? Our best answer is: "Learn as much as possible about the class of positions for which you've applied." The exam will test the knowledge, skills and abilities needed to do the work.

Your most valuable source of information about the position you want is the official exam announcement. This announcement lists the training and experience qualifications. Check these standards and apply only if you come reasonably close to meeting them. Many jurisdictions preview the written test in the exam announcement by including a section called "Knowledge and Abilities Required," "Scope of the Examination," or some similar heading. Here you will find out specifically what fields will be tested.

2) Choose appropriate study materials

If the position for which you are applying is technical or advanced, you will read more advanced, specialized material. If you are already familiar with the basic principles of your field, elementary textbooks would waste your time. Concentrate on advanced textbooks and technical periodicals. Think through the concepts and review difficult problems in your field.

These are all general sources. You can get more ideas on your own initiative, following these leads. For example, training manuals and publications of the government agency which employs workers in your field can be useful, particularly for technical and professional positions. A letter or visit to the government department involved may result in more specific study suggestions, and certainly will provide you with a more definite idea of the exact nature of the position you are seeking.

3) Study this book!

III. KINDS OF TESTS

Tests are used for purposes other than measuring knowledge and ability to perform specified duties. For some positions, it is equally important to test ability to make adjustments to new situations or to profit from training. In others, basic mental abilities not dependent on information are essential. Questions which test these things may not appear as pertinent to the duties of the position as those which test for knowledge and information. Yet they are often highly important parts of a fair examination. For very general questions, it is almost impossible to help you direct your study efforts. What we can do is to point out some of the more common of these general abilities needed in public service positions and describe some typical questions.

1) General information

Broad, general information has been found useful for predicting job success in some kinds of work. This is tested in a variety of ways, from vocabulary lists to questions about current events. Basic background in some field of work, such as sociology or economics, may be sampled in a group of questions. Often these are

- Dress comfortably – A written test is not a fashion show. You will be known by number and not by name, so wear something comfortable.
- Leave excess paraphernalia at home – Shopping bags and odd bundles will get in your way. You need bring only the items mentioned in the official notice you received; usually everything you need is provided. Do not bring reference books to the exam. They will only confuse those last minutes and be taken away from you when in the test room.
- Arrive somewhat ahead of time – If because of transportation schedules you must get there very early, bring a newspaper or magazine to take your mind off yourself while waiting.
- Locate the examination room – When you have found the proper room, you will be directed to the seat or part of the room where you will sit. Sometimes you are given a sheet of instructions to read while you are waiting. Do not fill out any forms until you are told to do so; just read them and be prepared.
- Relax and prepare to listen to the instructions
- If you have any physical problem that may keep you from doing your best, be sure to tell the test administrator. If you are sick or in poor health, you really cannot do your best on the exam. You can come back and take the test some other time.

VII. AT THE TEST

The day of the test is here and you have the test booklet in your hand. The temptation to get going is very strong. Caution! There is more to success than knowing the right answers. You must know how to identify your papers and understand variations in the type of short-answer question used in this particular examination. Follow these suggestions for maximum results from your efforts:

1) Cooperate with the monitor
The test administrator has a duty to create a situation in which you can be as much at ease as possible. He will give instructions, tell you when to begin, check to see that you are marking your answer sheet correctly, and so on. He is not there to guard you, although he will see that your competitors do not take unfair advantage. He wants to help you do your best.

2) Listen to all instructions
Don't jump the gun! Wait until you understand all directions. In most civil service tests you get more time than you need to answer the questions. So don't be in a hurry. Read each word of instructions until you clearly understand the meaning. Study the examples, listen to all announcements and follow directions. Ask questions if you do not understand what to do.

3) Identify your papers
Civil service exams are usually identified by number only. You will be assigned a number; you must not put your name on your test papers. Be sure to copy your number correctly. Since more than one exam may be given, copy your exact examination title.

4) Plan your time
Unless you are told that a test is a "speed" or "rate of work" test, speed itself is usually not important. Time enough to answer all the questions will be provided, but this

does not mean that you have all day. An overall time limit has been set. Divide the total time (in minutes) by the number of questions to determine the approximate time you have for each question.

5) Do not linger over difficult questions

If you come across a difficult question, mark it with a paper clip (useful to have along) and come back to it when you have been through the booklet. One caution if you do this – be sure to skip a number on your answer sheet as well. Check often to be sure that you have not lost your place and that you are marking in the row numbered the same as the question you are answering.

6) Read the questions

Be sure you know what the question asks! Many capable people are unsuccessful because they failed to *read* the questions correctly.

7) Answer all questions

Unless you have been instructed that a penalty will be deducted for incorrect answers, it is better to guess than to omit a question.

8) Speed tests

It is often better NOT to guess on speed tests. It has been found that on timed tests people are tempted to spend the last few seconds before time is called in marking answers at random – without even reading them – in the hope of picking up a few extra points. To discourage this practice, the instructions may warn you that your score will be "corrected" for guessing. That is, a penalty will be applied. The incorrect answers will be deducted from the correct ones, or some other penalty formula will be used.

9) Review your answers

If you finish before time is called, go back to the questions you guessed or omitted to give them further thought. Review other answers if you have time.

10) Return your test materials

If you are ready to leave before others have finished or time is called, take ALL your materials to the monitor and leave quietly. Never take any test material with you. The monitor can discover whose papers are not complete, and taking a test booklet may be grounds for disqualification.

VIII. EXAMINATION TECHNIQUES

1) Read the general instructions carefully. These are usually printed on the first page of the exam booklet. As a rule, these instructions refer to the timing of the examination; the fact that you should not start work until the signal and must stop work at a signal, etc. If there are any *special* instructions, such as a choice of questions to be answered, make sure that you note this instruction carefully.

2) When you are ready to start work on the examination, that is as soon as the signal has been given, read the instructions to each question booklet, underline any key words or phrases, such as *least, best, outline, describe*

and the like. In this way you will tend to answer as requested rather than discover on reviewing your paper that you *listed without describing*, that you selected the *worst* choice rather than the *best* choice, etc.

3) If the examination is of the objective or multiple-choice type – that is, each question will also give a series of possible answers: A, B, C or D, and you are called upon to select the best answer and write the letter next to that answer on your answer paper – it is advisable to start answering each question in turn. There may be anywhere from 50 to 100 such questions in the three or four hours allotted and you can see how much time would be taken if you read through all the questions before beginning to answer any. Furthermore, if you come across a question or group of questions which you know would be difficult to answer, it would undoubtedly affect your handling of all the other questions.

4) If the examination is of the essay type and contains but a few questions, it is a moot point as to whether you should read all the questions before starting to answer any one. Of course, if you are given a choice – say five out of seven and the like – then it is essential to read all the questions so you can eliminate the two that are most difficult. If, however, you are asked to answer all the questions, there may be danger in trying to answer the easiest one first because you may find that you will spend too much time on it. The best technique is to answer the first question, then proceed to the second, etc.

5) Time your answers. Before the exam begins, write down the time it started, then add the time allowed for the examination and write down the time it must be completed, then divide the time available somewhat as follows:
   - If 3-1/2 hours are allowed, that would be 210 minutes. If you have 80 objective-type questions, that would be an average of 2-1/2 minutes per question. Allow yourself no more than 2 minutes per question, or a total of 160 minutes, which will permit about 50 minutes to review.
   - If for the time allotment of 210 minutes there are 7 essay questions to answer, that would average about 30 minutes a question. Give yourself only 25 minutes per question so that you have about 35 minutes to review.

6) The most important instruction is to *read each question* and make sure you know what is wanted. The second most important instruction is to *time yourself properly* so that you answer every question. The third most important instruction is to *answer every question*. Guess if you have to but include something for each question. Remember that you will receive no credit for a blank and will probably receive some credit if you write something in answer to an essay question. If you guess a letter – say "B" for a multiple-choice question – you may have guessed right. If you leave a blank as an answer to a multiple-choice question, the examiners may respect your feelings but it will not add a point to your score. Some exams may penalize you for wrong answers, so in such cases *only*, you may not want to guess unless you have some basis for your answer.

7) Suggestions
   a. Objective-type questions
      1. Examine the question booklet for proper sequence of pages and questions
      2. Read all instructions carefully
      3. Skip any question which seems too difficult; return to it after all other questions have been answered
      4. Apportion your time properly; do not spend too much time on any single question or group of questions
      5. Note and underline key words – *all, most, fewest, least, best, worst, same, opposite,* etc.
      6. Pay particular attention to negatives
      7. Note unusual option, e.g., unduly long, short, complex, different or similar in content to the body of the question
      8. Observe the use of "hedging" words – *probably, may, most likely,* etc.
      9. Make sure that your answer is put next to the same number as the question
      10. Do not second-guess unless you have good reason to believe the second answer is definitely more correct
      11. Cross out original answer if you decide another answer is more accurate; do not erase until you are ready to hand your paper in
      12. Answer all questions; guess unless instructed otherwise
      13. Leave time for review

   b. Essay questions
      1. Read each question carefully
      2. Determine exactly what is wanted. Underline key words or phrases.
      3. Decide on outline or paragraph answer
      4. Include many different points and elements unless asked to develop any one or two points or elements
      5. Show impartiality by giving pros and cons unless directed to select one side only
      6. Make and write down any assumptions you find necessary to answer the questions
      7. Watch your English, grammar, punctuation and choice of words
      8. Time your answers; don't crowd material

8) Answering the essay question

Most essay questions can be answered by framing the specific response around several key words or ideas. Here are a few such key words or ideas:

M's: manpower, materials, methods, money, management
P's: purpose, program, policy, plan, procedure, practice, problems, pitfalls, personnel, public relations
a. Six basic steps in handling problems:
      1. Preliminary plan and background development
      2. Collect information, data and facts
      3. Analyze and interpret information, data and facts
      4. Analyze and develop solutions as well as make recommendations

5. Prepare report and sell recommendations
6. Install recommendations and follow up effectiveness

b. Pitfalls to avoid
1. *Taking things for granted* – A statement of the situation does not necessarily imply that each of the elements is necessarily true; for example, a complaint may be invalid and biased so that all that can be taken for granted is that a complaint has been registered
2. *Considering only one side of a situation* – Wherever possible, indicate several alternatives and then point out the reasons you selected the best one
3. *Failing to indicate follow up* – Whenever your answer indicates action on your part, make certain that you will take proper follow-up action to see how successful your recommendations, procedures or actions turn out to be
4. *Taking too long in answering any single question* – Remember to time your answers properly

EXAMINATION SECTION

EXAMINATION SECTION
TEST 1

DIRECTIONS: Each question or incomplete statement is followed by several suggested answers or completions. Select the one the BEST answers the question or completes the statement. *PRINT THE LETTER OF THE CORRECT ANSWER IN THE SPACE AT THE RIGHT.*

1. Which of the following is an example of primary health education?   1._____

    A.   Helping clients with maturity-onset diabetes to reverse imbalances in blood sugar
    B.   Teaching community members about the elements of an adequate and balanced diet
    C.   Helping a diabetic who has lost a limb to amputation how to maximize his potential for healthy living
    D.   Teaching overweight clients how to adjust their diet in order to lose weight

2. Which of the following is a disadvantage associated with the use of videotapes for instruction or promotion?   2._____

    A.   Not appropriate for group settings
    B.   Expensive to produce
    C.   Distribution is complicated
    D.   Low probability of audience identification with subjects

3. The foundation of any community health promotion program is generally considered to be   3._____

    A.   remediation
    B.   advocacy
    C.   prevention
    D.   maintenance

4. When writing materials for adults with limited reading skills, readability tests performed on the materials should indicate a level of about _____ grade.   4._____

    A. 3rd
    B. 5th
    C. 7th
    D. 9th

5. To spread the word about a health promotion program, a health educator wants to make use of a local television station. Which of the following personnel would probably be LEAST useful as a contact?   5._____

    A.   Commentator
    B.   Health/medical reporter
    C.   News assignment editor
    D.   Talk show producer/host

6. In a large urban area, members of a geographically concentrated Chinese immigrant community seem to suffer disproportionately from foodborne illnesses. In the past, adults from this community have proven reluctant to share personal opinions or feelings in front of others. A health educator, hoping to reduce the risk of these kinds of illnesses, launches a needs assessment program to determine whether a program should be designed for this group. Which of the following approaches to needs assessment is probably LEAST appropriate for this community?

    A. Focus group
    B. Written survey
    C. Literature review
    D. Observation

6.____

7. A county health department has observed that educational print materials about breast cancer, which the department received from the state health administration, are written at too high a reading level and are not culturally appropriate for the older, low-income Asian American women in the department's target community. For health educators at the department, the most appropriate next step would be to

    A. hire a professional graphic artist to create illustrations of older Asian American women to accompany the materials
    B. develop materials for other media, such as visuals or radio announcements
    C. conduct focus groups to identify appropriate communication channels, credible information sources, and the acceptability of breast cancer materials
    D. simplify the text of the materials

7.____

8. Prior to the full implementation of a marketing strategy for health education services, it will be necessary for program designers to conduct _____ research.

    A. experimental
    B. ethnographic
    C. longitudinal
    D. formative

8.____

9. As a funding source for health education programs, corporate grants

    A. usually require a more formal proposal preparation than a foundation grant
    B. may take the form of matching gifts
    C. are issued through an RFP or RFA process
    D. are typically easier to obtain than foundation grants

9.____

10. Among the cultural group of clients broadly classified as "Native American," a health educator should expect to find the most traditional of these to be characterized by

    A. patriarchal family systems
    B. independence and individualism
    C. acceptance of death as part of the natural life cycle
    D. a focus on the nuclear family

10.____

11. Which of the following is NOT a problems or barrier involved in performing an impact analysis of a health education program?

    A. Impact evaluations involve extended commitment from members of the agency.
    B. They are not as comprehensive or thorough as other forms of evaluation.

11.____

C. They frequently rely on other strategies in addition to communication.
D. Results often cannot be directly related to the effects of a program.

12. When collecting the morbidity data of a community, a health educator must keep in mind that   12.____

    A. reporting any listed diagnosis does not accurately represent the disease burden associated with a condition
    B. reporting only primary diagnosis data will often underrepresent the actual prevalence of a particular disease
    C. it is usually difficult to obtain hospital discharge data
    D. morbidity data should be collected independent of any opinion data collected among community members

13. The most successful worksite health education programs will typically include a(n)   13.____

    A. co-enrollment and participation by employees of other local companies
    B. advisory or coordinating committee composed of employees from various levels and departments
    C. built-in referral service
    D. steering committee composed of health education professionals from various levels and departments in the local community

14. To some degree, a health educator usually tries to include community members in the planning process of a health education program. When possible, a health educator should involve community members in   14.____
        I. adapting or developing materials
       II. choosing appropriate strategies to reach the intended audience
      III. evaluating the program
      IV. developing the health messages

    A. I and IV
    B. II only
    C. II, III and IV
    D. I, II, III and IV

15. As a general rule, the budget considerations for a health education program that is planned on an ongoing basis should reflect a_____ -year projection   15.____

    A. 1
    B. 3
    C. 5
    D. 10

16. Pre-testing health messages and materials is considered to be essential as a condition for acceptance in a program. However, it does have limitations. The most significant of these is that pre-testing   16.____

    A. is of little use when messages contain especially sensitive or controversial content
    B. can assess emotional responses, but does little to demonstrate the extent of client comprehension
    C. is essentially qualitative in nature, and does not involve statistical precision
    D. has no provision for determining the perceived personal relevance of messages

17. Of the following steps in establishing a community health education program, which should typically occur LAST?

    A. Promoting the organization
    B. Conducting a needs analysis
    C. Recruiting volunteers
    D. Developing job descriptions

17.____

18. Each of the following is a guideline to be used in adapting a health education program to a different culture, EXCEPT

    A. trying to personalize the delivery of the program, rather than use the mass-media approach
    B. asking community members to choose a name for the program
    C. organizing health education activities around recreational activities or community celebrations
    D. providing word-for-word translations of audio, video, or written program materials

18.____

19. A health educator is helping to plan a school health center for a large and culturally diverse urban high school. The most compelling reason to adopt a school-based, rather than school-linked, structure for this school health center is the

    A. avoidance of professional turf wars
    B. issue of legal liability
    C. greater school control over service delivery
    D. low health-seeking behavior of adolescents

19.____

20. Which of the following is NOT a risk factor associated with heart disease?

    A. High blood cholesterol
    B. Alcohol abuse
    C. Environmental factors
    D. Hypertension

20.____

21. The most significant criticism of the educational approach to health promotion is that programs and personnel

    A. focus too much on individuals and does little to alter their environment
    B. impose medical values on the client
    C. is likely to induce feelings of guilt if clients choose not to follow prescribed regimes
    D. assumes that clients believe that health "experts" know best

21.____

22. At a bare minimum, a comprehensive health promotion program at a major worksite should include each of the following activities, EXCEPT

    A. group smoking cessation programs
    B. support groups of various types
    C. blood pressure control programs
    D. health education classes on selected topics

22.____

23. Which of the following steps in developing a successful health education program would typically be performed FIRST?

    A. Writing a mission statement
    B. Writing goals and objectives
    C. Inventory of organizational resources
    D. Needs assessment

23.____

24. In dealing with largely ethnic communities, it is helpful for the health educator to recognize the differences between other cultures and the dominant Anglo-American culture. Which of the following is NOT typically identified as a generalized Anglo-American cultural trait?

    A. Formality
    B. Human equality
    C. Practicality and efficiency
    D. Individualism and privacy

24.____

25. A community's health education needs are assessed directly through the value judgements of the health educator and other professionals. This is an example of _____ need.

    A. expressed
    B. normative
    C. felt
    D. comparative

25.____

KEY (CORRECT ANSWERS)

1.	B		11.	B
2.	B		12.	B
3.	C		13.	B
4.	B		14.	D
5.	A		15.	B
6.	A		16.	C
7.	C		17.	C
8.	D		18.	D
9.	B		19.	D
10.	C		20.	C

21.	A
22.	B
23.	A
24.	A
25.	B

TEST 2

DIRECTIONS: Each question or incomplete statement is followed by several suggested answers or completions. Select the one the BEST answers the question or completes the statement. *PRINT THE LETTER OF THE CORRECT ANSWER IN THE SPACE AT THE RIGHT.*

1. Which of the following types of information is LEAST likely to be produced by the outcome evaluation of a health education program?

   A. Long-term maintenance of desired behavior
   B. Policies initiated or other institutional changes made
   C. Expressed intentions of the target clientele
   D. Knowledge and attitude changes

   1.____

2. In dealing with ethnic communities, it is helpful for the health educator to recognize the differences between other cultures and the dominant Anglo-American culture. Which of the following is typically identified as a generalized Anglo-American cultural trait?

   A. Orientation toward being, rather than action or work
   B. Emphasis on duration of life, rather than overall quality
   C. Cooperation, rather than competition
   D. Tradition, rather than change

   2.____

3. Which of the following is NOT a risk factor typically associated with pneumonia or influenza?

   A. Tobacco use
   B. Health care access
   C. Workplace hazards
   D. Biological factors

   3.____

4. For the health educator, the most significant difference between grants and contracts as funding sources for programs is that grants

   A. allow more creativity and flexibility in a particular project
   B. are more likely to be awarded to unsolicited proposals
   C. provide 100 percent funding for initiatives
   D. usually go to for-profit organizations

   4.____

5. Which of the following is an advantage associated with the use of interactive media for instruction or promotion?

   A. Applicability to group settings
   B. Minimal computer literacy requirements of learners
   C. Minimal staff support requirements
   D. Requires little technical skill to develop

   5.____

6. In the context of health promotion, the purposes of health education include each of the following, EXCEPT providing

   A. awareness
   C. advocacy
   B. maintenance
   D. prevention

   6.____

7. A focus group has convened as part of a health educator's community assessment. Of the following, the LEAST useful or appropriate question for the educator to ask group members would be

    7.____

    A. How do you feel about the general quality of life for people in this community?
    B. Do you agree that there are people in this community who would benefit from changing certain behaviors?
    C. How have people responded in the past to health education programs?
    D. What do you think about the idea of promoting an exercise class for seniors?

8. The first phase of the PRECEDE model of planning health education is the _____ diagnosis.

    8.____

    A. epidemiological
    B. educational
    C. behavioral
    D. administrative

9. When working one-one-one or in small groups with clients from different cultures, a health educator should remember that in general, people from _____ communities will prefer the greatest distance between themselves and people with whom they are speaking.

    9.____

    A. African-American
    B. Hispanic-American
    C. Anglo-American
    D. Asian-American

10. Which of the following would NOT be a guideline for presenting educational programs to groups of older adults?

    10.____

    A. Encourage participation, such as answering questions, role-playing, and real-life scenarios
    B. Begin presentations with an introductory overview.
    C. Adjust the environment to accommodate sensory deficits that are common among older people.
    D. Plan to present information in 1 - to 2-hour blocks, and leave time for questioning.

11. A 60-year-old male with an enlarged prostate returns to his to a physician because he's had abdominal pain for two days. Four days ago, his physician prescribed Benadryl for his allergies. After he began to take Benadryl, the man's urine slowed down and then he developed abdominal pain. This case is an example of

    11.____

    A. iatrogenesis
    B. blaming the victim
    C. secondary morbidity
    D. treating symptoms, rather than the cause

12. To pre-test a draft copy of a flier that will distributed during a cancer awareness work-   12.____
shop, a health educator mails the flier directly to a sampling of community members,
along with a questionnaire about its content and format. The potential disadvantages of
using the self-administered questionnaire include
    I.   low response rates
    II. uncontrolled exposure to draft materials
    III. typically require follow-up
    IV. extended time lapse between production and responses

    A. I and II
    B. II and IV
    C. III only
    D. I, II, III and IV

13. In the coalition model of health education and promotion, which of the following organiza-   13.____
tions usually consists of citizens who are appointed by official bodies?

    A. Commissions
    B. Advisory committees
    C. Task forces
    D. Consortia/alliances

14. Guidelines for the composition of print materials as health instruction media include   14.____
    I.   Abbreviations and acronyms should be used for the purpose of simplicity
    II. Text should be written in active, not passive, voice
    III. Graphics should be immediately identifiable
    IV. No type smaller than 10-point should be used

    A. I only
    B. II and IV
    C. II, III and IV
    D. I, II, III and IV

15. As part of a community assessment, a health educator wants to compile information on   15.____
primary care services and community services. As a source of this information, the first
and best choice would be

    A. the state department of human services
    B. the state department of health
    C. the state department of aging
    D. local information and referral service inventories

16. As a mass media channel for the communication of a health-related message or public   16.____
service announcement, television

    A. is an inexpensive and relatively easy way to get a message out
    B. is most likely to reach low-income and other audiences who are unlikely to turn to
       health sources for help
    C. involves a relatively high degree of client attention and involvement
    D. allows for the communication of more complex health issues or behaviors

17. Which of the following methods for recruiting volunteers for a health education program is generally LEAST effective?   17.____

    A. Articles placed in business/community newsletters
    B. Person-to-person contact
    C. News releases/public service announcements
    D. Classified advertising

18. A health educator designs a number of goals for his substance abuse treatment program, beginning at the individual consciousness level and moving to social change. The educator will have accomplished a behavior change goal if, after completing the program, a client can say that he   18.____

    A. now drinks less than he used to
    B. understands that drinking too much is bad for him
    C. is aware that he is drinking too much
    D. finds that soft drinks are becoming more socially acceptable in bars and clubs

19. The first step in any community assessment performed prior to the design of a health education program is usually a(n)   19.____

    A. oral survey
    B. literature review
    C. focus group
    D. community observation

20. When developing and writing specific objectives, it is important to remember that each objective must include   20.____
    I. the performance or action being stated
    II. a measurable factor
    III. a time element
    IV. a standard of performance or condition

    A. I and II
    B. I, II and IV
    C. II and IV
    D. I, II, III and IV

21. Which of the following activities would MOST likely be associated with the social change model of health education?   21.____

    A. Limiting and challenging cigarette advertising and sports sponsorship
    B. Persuasive education to prevent non-smokers from starting
    C. Helping clients to learn how to stop smoking if they want to
    D. Screening clients for tobacco-related illnesses

22. Health promotion and health education programs should NOT be developed to   22.____

    A. include interventions that will focus on a single risk factor
    B. operate in ways that can be specifically measured and evaluated
    C. apply methods that are universally proven among different settings
    D. conform to the needs and preferences of the target group(s)

23. A modestly-funded local health agency wants to perform an outcome analysis of the pub-   23.____
licity campaign for its vaccination program. Which of the following procedures would be
most appropriate?

    A. Telephone survey of self-reported behavior
    B. Focus groups
    C. Calculation of the percentage of the target audience who participated
    D. Study of long-term disease trends

24. The leading cause of death and injury of children under 12 in the United States is   24.____

    A. violence outside the home
    B. home health hazards
    C. automobile accidents
    D. abuse and neglect

25. Which of the following is LEAST likely to be successful as a means of assessing employ-   25.____
ees' health needs in a worksite wellness outreach?

    A. Asking for health risk information including smoking, weight, exercise, etc.
    B. Surveying employees about their interest in wellness programs
    C. Take-home, self-administered health-risk appraisals
    D. Measuring blood pressure and cholesterol

KEY (CORRECT ANSWERS)

1.	A	11.	A
2.	B	12.	D
3.	C	13.	A
4.	A	14.	C
5.	C	15.	D
6.	C	16.	B
7.	B	17.	D
8.	A	18.	A
9.	D	19.	B
10.	D	20.	D

21.	A
22.	C
23.	C
24.	B
25.	C

TEST 3

DIRECTIONS: Each question or incomplete statement is followed by several suggested answers or completions. Select the one the BEST answers the question or completes the statement. *PRINT THE LETTER OF THE CORRECT ANSWER IN THE SPACE AT THE RIGHT.*

1. As part of the needs assessment process, a health educator attempts to assemble a community profile. In this process, advantages of using geographic and political boundaries in defining a community include
    I.   easier data collection
    II. greater likelihood of influencing the use of government resources and policies to address priority health problems
    III. greater likelihood of a shared identity among community members
    IV. increased probability of common demographic trends

    A. I only
    B. I and II
    C. II, III and IV
    D. I, II, III and IV

1.____

2. Of the following, which element of a health education program is MOST likely to have the greatest impact on producing lasting changes?

    A. Preventing injury and disease
    B. Changing health behaviors
    C. Enhancing awareness of positive health habits
    D. Creating a supportive environment for good health practices

2.____

3. According to the PATCH model of health education planning developed by the Centers for Disease Control and prevention, five elements are considered critical to the success of any community health education process. Which of the following is NOT one of these?

    A. Data are used to guide the development of programs
    B. The capacity of community members to promote health should be increased.
    C. Evaluation should emphasize feedback and improvement.
    D. Participants develop a solution-focused approach to solving specific health problems.

3.____

4. Before deciding upon a means of instruction, a health educator should know that people tend to retain 90 percent of what they

    A. do and say
    B. see and hear
    C. read
    D. say

4.____

5. When developing materials for clients with limited reading skills, it is important to remember that low-literacy clients typically

    A. depend on auditory cues to clarify and interpret words
    B. rely on a broad set of inferences outside their personal experience when reading

5.____

    C.   have longer attention spans than expected
    D.   have difficulty understanding complex ideas, especially those with several elements

6.   A health educator is participating in the writing of a grant proposal for a risk reduction program among an urban immigrant community. Typically, the cover letter that accompanies a proposal for a government or foundation grant should include a brief explanation of each of the following, EXCEPT the   6.____

    A.   total funding requirement
    B.   methods for evaluating program success
    C.   purpose of the project
    D.   project's relevance to the foundation's or agency's interest

7.   Which of the following would be a useful resource for discovering a local wellness council?   7.____

    I.   Local chamber of commerce
    II.   Wellness Councils of America (WELCOA)
    III. Local recreation department
    IV. YMCA of USA

    A.   I and II
    B.   II and III
    C.   III only
    D.   I, II, III and IV

8.   Advantages associated with the coalition model of health education and promotion include each of the following, EXCEPT   8.____

    A.   enhanced credibility
    B.   appropriateness for brief, task-based interventions
    C.   conservation of community resources
    D.   broader reach within a community

9.   In a written objective for a health promotion program, which of the following verbs would be LEAST appropriate for describing a client outcome?   9.____

    A.   Classify
    B.   Interpret
    C.   Know
    D.   Define

10. A health educator wants to study the relationships between age, gender, ethnic background and two dependent variables: drug use and sexual behavior. The type of study to be conducted will be   10.____

    A.   ex post facto
    B.   multivariate
    C.   pre-test/post-test
    D.   longitudinal

11. Which of the following activities would MOST likely be associated with the educational model of health education?   11.____

    A. Lobbying for a no-smoking policy in public places.
    B. Encouraging people to seek early detection and treatment of smoking-related disorders.
    C. Helping clients to explore their own values and attitudes about smoking.
    D. Responding to clients' self-identified concern with smoking as a health issue with printed educational materials.

12. Which of the following needs assessment activities is MOST likely to yield only quantitative data?   12.____

    A. Written survey
    B. Observation
    C. Focus group
    D. In-depth interview

13. As a mass media channel for the communication of a health-related message or public service announcement, radio does NOT   13.____

    A. generally reach fewer people than television
    B. offer a greater potential for audience targeting than television
    C. involve relatively high production and distribution expenses
    D. offer the opportunity for direct audience involvement

14. When designing a program targeted to African-American clients, a health educator should know that African-American parenting styles generally result in each of the following, EXCEPT that children   14.____

    A. have less body contact (breast feeding, holding, etc.) with their parents than most other American children.
    B. are taught to comply with requests that do not have immediate tangible rewards
    C. are taught that there is a supreme being that is greater than themselves
    D. learn the responsibility of caring for other children

15. A health educator wants to test the readability of some written instructional materials he has designed for a stop-smoking seminar. The quickest and most efficient way to do this would be to   15.____

    A. have the materials screened by colleagues
    B. consult with a reading instructor from the community
    C. give the materials to volunteers who are representative of the target population, and follow up with comprehension questions
    D. use the Fry scale

16. Of the following risk factors, which plays a contributing role in ALL leading causes of death in America?   16.____

    A. Diet
    B. Stress
    C. Substance abuse
    D. Health care access

17. In order to secure volunteers to help implement a health education program, the best approach is usually to emphasize the

    A. rewards of participating in the program
    B. numbers of children and infants who will benefit from the program
    C. risk factors in the community that need to be changed
    D. moral imperative of improving community health

17.____

18. Which of the following is an example of tertiary health education?

    A. Campaigning for safer roads and stricter enforcement of traffic laws
    B. Conducting a smoking cessation workshop in a group format
    C. Teaching a client with juvenile-onset diabetes how to adjust eating habits
    D. Teaching basic skin care to clients with acne.

18.____

19. The basic purpose of a formative program evaluation is to

    A. document the short-term results of the program
    B. maximize the chance for program success before the communication activity starts
    C. help determine whether outcomes were in fact produced by elements of the program
    D. obtain descriptive data on a project

19.____

20. A health educator decides that in conducting a course for teenage alcoholics on the health risks associated with drinking, she will adopt an authoritarian communication style. The most likely positive outcome associated with this approach is that clients will

    A. appreciate others' own rights and opinions about how to solve problems
    B. be encouraged to explore their feelings more freely and to be creative about finding solutions
    C. be given clear guidance on how to resolve their problems
    D. feel protected from harm and able to cope with their problems

20.____

21. Which of the following is LEAST likely to be successful as a means of recruiting employees for a worksite wellness outreach?

    A. On-the-spot sign-ups during screenings
    B. Follow-up personal visits to workstations or job sites
    C. Individual telephone calls
    D. Persistent use of the media and individual mailings

21.____

22. In innovation-diffusion theory, an individual who influences the client's decision in a more desirable direction is known as a(n)

    A. innovator
    B. motivator
    C. change agent
    D. impeller

22.____

23. A health agency has composed draft materials for a nutrition awareness program, and   23._____
wants to hear what members of the community think of the materials. The coordinator
schedules individual interviews with a number of people who represent different sub-
groups in the community. The advantages associated with the individual interview as a
program pre-test include

    I.   rapid response analysis
    II. small time requirements
    III. the ability to explore emotional or complex issues
    IV. the ability to communicate with hard-to-reach audiences

    A. I and II
    B. II, III and IV
    C. III and IV
    D. I, II, III and IV

24. According to the Society for Public Health Education's (SOPHE) code of ethics, each of   24._____
the following is a responsibility of a health educator, EXCEPT to

    A. further health education through applied research
    B. share skills and experience with students and colleagues
    C. advocate for change and legislation, and speak out on issues harmful to public
       health
    D. guide communities in their choices through selective and judicious provision of
       information

25. The most significant advantage of the medical model of health education is that it   25._____

    A. takes into account the social factors that influence client behaviors
    B. encourages clients to seek and discover information about healthy lifestyle choices
    C. assumes that individual behavior is the primary cause of ill health
    D. draws on the knowledge of trained professionals to identify the most effective
       mode of intervention

KEY (CORRECT ANSWERS)

1.	B		11.	C
2.	D		12.	A
3.	D		13.	C
4.	A		14.	A
5.	D		15.	D
6.	B		16.	D
7.	A		17.	A
8.	B		18.	C
9.	C		19.	B
10.	B		20.	C

21.	D
22.	C
23.	C
24.	D
25.	D

———

EXAMINATION SECTION
TEST 1

DIRECTIONS: Each question or incomplete statement is followed by several suggested answers or completions. Select the one the BEST answers the question or completes the statement. *PRINT THE LETTER OF THE CORRECT ANSWER IN THE SPACE AT THE RIGHT.*

1. A health educator helps collect data for an epidemiological study that will examine the relationship, during the months of December and January, between the incidence of influenza in a community and the behaviors of the community members. The type of study to be conducted will be

    A. longitudinal
    B. ex post facto
    C. cross-sectional
    D. pre-test/post-test

1.____

2. In a worksite wellness program, which of the following is LEAST likely to help employees change their health risks?

    A. The use of "engagement" strategies that are individually designed
    B. A solid and focused array of health improvement classes and seminars
    C. Repeated follow-up contacts after programs or classes have ended
    D. Persistent, personalized outreach to at-risk employees

2.____

3. The final phase of the PRECEDE model of planning health education is the _____ diagnosis.

    A. behavioral
    B. administrative
    C. educational
    D. social

3.____

4. Typically, a health promotion effort in a community should begin with a(n)

    A. enhancement of community awareness about the program
    B. behavioral change strategy
    C. screening and appraisal of health risks
    D. socioemotional intervention

4.____

5. Role-playing exercises are sometimes a useful means of instruction in health education. Generally, a disadvantage associated with this activity is that it

    A. focuses on a narrow band of skills
    B. tends to truncate discussions
    C. makes learning more abstract
    D. requires a well-trained facilitator

5.____

6. In researching a community profile, which of the following items of information would probably be LEAST useful to a health educator?

    A. Average educational level of residents
    B. Age distribution

6.____

C. Political affiliations
D. Average household income

7. A health educator decides that in conducting a course for young teenagers on the dangers of unprotected sex, he will adopt a paternalistic communication style. A potential disadvantage associated with this decision is that

    A. attention is often diverted from real problems
    B. clients may become reluctant to take independent action
    C. clients may become likely to rebel or reject the views of the health educator
    D. the health educator may be perceived as neither supportive nor caring

7.____

8. To help conduct effective meetings, health educators and other program members should

    A. begin only when all members of the group are present
    B. record minutes of each meeting and distribute them before the next
    C. take collective responsibility for tasks and deadlines
    D. let people raise issues that are important to them, even if they are not on the agenda

8.____

9. Though the cultural groups that make up the broad category known as "Asian American" are varied in their beliefs and customs, it should generally be expected that first-generation immigrants from Asia will share a set of traditional values and behavior. Which of the following would be LEAST likely to be included in these values and behaviors?

    A. Assertive help-seeking in time of need
    B. Blame of self for failure
    C. Control of strong feelings
    D. Respect for authority

9.____

10. As a general rule, sentences that appear in a health education brochure should each contain about _____ or fewer words.

    A. 8
    B. 12
    C. 17
    D. 25

10.____

11. A health educator is participating in the writing of a grant proposal for a hygiene awareness program for migrant workers. Typically, the body of a proposal should FIRST contain

    A. specific goals and objectives of the program
    B. a description of the target population
    C. an itemized budget for the program, including all expenses and a justification for each
    D. a one-page summary of the entire proposal

11.____

12. When defining and organizing a message for an adult audience with limited reading skills, a health educator should NOT

    A. put the most important information in the middle of the presentation
    B. present one idea on a single page, or two facing pages

12.____

C. frequently summarize or repeat concepts
D. start with the completed idea one wants understood, then provide a breakdown or explanation

13. Which of the following theories would be MOST helpful in designing a program for treating alcohol abuse?

13.____

   A. Consensus
   B. Innovation-diffusion
   C. Conflict
   D. Self-regulation

14. As a mass media channel for the communication of a health-related message or public service announcement, magazines

14.____

   A. are more approachable and involve easier placement of PSAs than audiovisual media
   B. do not enable agencies to more specifically target segments of the public
   C. can explain more complex health issues and behaviors
   D. generally involve passive consumption

15. Which of the following is a risk factor associated with stroke?

15.____

   A. Alcohol abuse
   B. Obesity
   C. Home hazards
   D. Infectious agents

16. Before deciding upon a means of instruction, a health educator should know that people generally retain only about 10 percent of content that they

16.____

   A. say
   B. read
   C. do
   D. hear

17. For participants in a breast and cervical cancer control program, a health educator adapted a low-literacy flier developed by another organization. The flier was pre-tested among community members, and found to be written at the appropriate level. Staff at the agency observed that women in the program, after receiving the fliers, folded them to fit them in their purses, and many women left the fliers behind in the clinic. The most appropriate next step would be to

17.____

   A. conduct a focus group to discover what kind of format women would prefer for written information
   B. modify the format but keep the original text, to produce a flier that will fit into a woman's purse
   C. discontinue production of the fliers, and instead rely on visual presentation of the material on-site
   D. monitor the women as they leave the clinic and encourage them to take the flier with them

18. As part of a community assessment, a health educator wants to conduct a focus group interview. The ideal number of members to participate in this sort of group is usually about

    18.____

    A. 3 to 5
    B. 4 to 8
    C. 10 to 12
    D. 15 to 20

19. In the client-centered model of health education, interventions are best described as

    19.____

    A. promotion of medical interventions to prevent or alleviate ill health
    B. instruction about the causes and effects of health-demoting factors
    C. changing clients' attitudes and behaviors to promote the adoption of a healthier lifestyle
    D. collaborations with clients to identify and act on health-related concerns

20. Each of the following is a guideline that should be used in acquiring information from clients who are of different cultural or language backgrounds, EXCEPT

    20.____

    A. asking questions in the exact same way repeatedly, to ensure understanding
    B. adjusting the style of the interaction to reflect differences in age between oneself and the client
    C. establishing rapport and showing genuine warm concern for the client, to build trust
    D. using open-ended questions to increase the amount of information obtained

21. The local newspaper has just run a story about a homeless encampment near the downtown area of a small city. An educator with the local health agency wants to write a letter to the editor of the paper, in order to draw attention to the services it offers to homeless people in the community. Guidelines for writing letters to be printed on the editorial page include

    21.____

    I.   the most important point should be made at the end of the letter
    II. letters should be saved for the most important issues
    III. letters should be signed by an officer of the organization
    IV. they should be no longer than 50-100 words

    A. I and II
    B. II and III
    C. III and IV
    D. I, II, III and IV

22. The lead agency in a coalition for health education and promotion should usually expect extensive staff demands in each of the following areas, EXCEPT

    22.____

    A. clerical
    B. service delivery
    C. fund-raising
    D. research and fact gathering

23. A health agency conducts a readability test on one of its brochures. This is a(n) _____ 23._____
evaluation of a health education procedure.

  A. impact
  B. process
  C. outcome
  D. formative

24. Most nationwide initiatives focusing on public health, such as Healthy People 2000, place 24._____
the highest priority on

  A. physical activity and fitness
  B. family planning
  C. occupational safety and health
  D. violent and abusive behavior

25. A health educator designs a number of goals for his exercise education program, begin- 25._____
ning at the individual consciousness level and moving to social change. The educator will
have accomplished a decision-making change goal if, after completing the program, a client can say that she

  A. feels unfit because she gets out of breath easily
  B. will take fitness classes
  C. states the belief that she would feel better if she exercised more
  D. now goes to the gym regularly and is generally more physically active

KEY (CORRECT ANSWERS)

1.	C	11.	D	
2.	B	12.	A	
3.	B	13.	D	
4.	C	14.	C	
5.	D	15.	A	
6.	C	16.	B	
7.	B	17.	B	
8.	B	18.	C	
9.	A	19.	D	
10.	C	20.	A	

21. B
22. B
23. D
24. A
25. B

TEST 2

DIRECTIONS: Each question or incomplete statement is followed by several suggested answers or completions. Select the one the BEST answers the question or completes the statement. *PRINT THE LETTER OF THE CORRECT ANSWER IN THE SPACE AT THE RIGHT.*

1. Which of the following is an example of secondary health education?   1.____

   A. Demonstrating the proper installation of a child car seat
   B. Explaining to a group of teens how to avoid contracting sexually transmitted diseases such as AIDS
   C. Showing clients how to give first aid after an accident
   D. Teaching a client with food allergies how to adjust eating habits to ensure minimum complications

2. A health educator wants to print a brochure on safe sex to be distributed among local teenagers. The educator should know that the greatest expense involved in printing materials is   2.____

   A. making the printing plates
   B. paper
   C. distribution costs
   D. original artwork or graphics

3. In the beginning phase of a health education program, a good needs assessment process can help the program designers to do each of the following, EXCEPT to   3.____

   A. identify which programs to implement first
   B. identify the types of programs needed
   C. establish a set of baseline data to demonstrate later improvements
   D. establish incentives for behavioral change

4. The most common mistake health educators make in designing a worksite wellness program is to   4.____

   A. depend solely on a schedule of classes for health improvement intervention
   B. focus only on at-risk employees
   C. use the "menu approach" to offering a variety of programs
   D. spend too much time tracking down employees to persuade them to take part in programs or classes

5. A health educator working in a Hispanic/Latino community should remember that the diverse Hispanic cultures in America tend to share some common values and behaviors. Which of the following is NOT one of these?   5.____

   A. Family as the primary source of emotional and psychological support.
   B. Matriarchal family structures.
   C. Consultation with several family members before seeking health care.
   D. Modesty and personal privacy.

6. Which of the following interventions does NOT conform to the medical model of health education?   6.____

    A. Persuading parents to bring their children in for vaccinations
    B. Teaching a course on how to care for teeth and gums
    C. Participating in a self-help group to discuss the issue of menopause
    D. Screening middle-aged men for high blood pressure

7. Of the following, which element should typically appear FIRST in the body of a proposal for the funding of a public health education program?   7.____

    A. The specific methods that will be used to meet program objectives-approach, action plan, timeline
    B. Process and outcome measures to be used in evaluating project success
    C. Brief background of the problem in the community, with supporting data
    D. The management plan for the project, including key staff members and their roles

8. At the local high school, a health educator is conducting a workshop on the dangers of certain commonly abused drugs to a group of Asian immigrant parents. The health educator is aware that English is a second language for many of the parents. Each of the following is a strategy that will help the educator overcome this language barrier in presenting information, EXCEPT   8.____

    A. speaking more loudly
    B. using images, gestures, and simple written instructions that may be understood by relatives
    C. speaking slowly and enunciating clearly
    D. repeating sentences in the same words if it's been misunderstood

9. A person who takes the structuralist view of behavior and social change will probably focus his or her efforts on the   9.____

    A. laws, codes, zoning ordinances, and taxation of the community
    B. sense of shared purpose among community members
    C. biomedical causes of a disease or disorder
    D. individual's motivation for change

10. When defining and organizing a written message for an adult audience with limited reading skills, a health educator's sentences should   10.____

    A. include vivid descriptive phrases to add interest
    B. average 8 to 10 words in length
    C. have roughly the same rhythm
    D. be written in the passive voice

11. In researching a community profile, most of the information can be obtained from the data collected by the   11.____

    A. local hospitals
    B. state and local social service departments
    C. chambers of commerce
    D. federal Bureau of the Census

12. When deciding whether to use visuals as part of health instruction, the primary consideration should be whether they   12.____

    A. enhance the message, rather than compete with it
    B. illustrate key concepts
    C. stimulate learner interest
    D. are culturally appropriate

13. The probability for learning in a health education program is likely to be enhanced when the following principles are used in program design: 13.____
    I. Program content is relevant to the learner, and is perceived by the learner to be relevant.
    II. Instructional methods that stimulate the widest variety of senses will generally be most effective.
    III. Concepts should be reviewed and repeated several times during instruction.
    IV. Instruction should move from the unknown to the known.

    A. I and IV
    B. I, II and III
    C. II and III
    D. I, II, III and IV

14. Which of the following is MOST likely to be a kind of formative evaluation used for a health education program?   14.____

    A. Studies of public behavior/health change
    B. Assessment of target audience for knowledge gain
    C. Calculation of percentage of target audience participating
    D. Focus group

15. In social marketing theory, the best example of a "channel gatekeeper" would be a   15.____

    A. mother of a large urban family
    B. postal carrier
    C. human resources manager at a large corporation
    D. social worker specializing in substance abuse

16. A health agency plans to publish its own nutrition handbook. Guidelines for the visual design of such a publication include   16.____
    I. Concepts that belong together or have similarities should be boxed in.
    II. Narrow columns, rather than full-page-wide text, should be used.
    III. When paragraphs are short, do not indent
    IV. If possible, margins should be wider at the bottom than at the top of the page.

    A. I only
    B. I and IV
    C. II and III
    D. I, II, III and IV

17. Which of the following is NOT a risk factor associated with cirrhosis?   17.____

    A. Infectious agents
    B. High blood cholesterol

    C.   Alcohol abuse
    D.   Biological factors

18.   Which of the following types of funding is MOST likely to be awarded for a program that   18._____
        originates with the funding source?

    A.   Grant
    B.   Public funds
    C.   Private funds
    D.   Contract

19.   The PROCEED model of planning health education programs adds each of the following   19._____
        procedures to the PRECEDE model, EXCEPT assessment of

    A.   budgetary and staff resources required
    B.   barriers to overcome in delivering health education
    C.   predisposing, enabling, and reinforcing factors among community members
    D.   policies that can be used to support the program

20.   Theatrical or dramatization exercises are sometimes a useful means of instruction in   20._____
        health education. Generally, a disadvantage associated with this activity is that it

    A.   may make some participants uncomfortable
    B.   stimulates participants' emotions
    C.   distracts from the real purpose of the program
    D.   may make issues seem artificial or contrived

21.   Which of the following questions would be MOST likely to appear in the formative evalua-   21._____
        tion of a health education program?

    A.   Did the media organizations that the agency contacted change their practices to
           include photos of safe bicycling?
    B.   How many agency-sponsored activities received coverage in the local press?
    C.   How many members actively monitored the local media on a regular basis?
    D.   How many parents were influenced to buy bicycle helmets after reading the
           agency's press releases?

22.   A health educator wants to draw attention to a new program by placing an op-ed piece   22._____
        about AIDS awareness in the local newspaper. The ideal length for such a piece would
        be about _____ words.

    A.   100
    B.   300
    C.   800
    D.   1200

23.   Of the following areas for change, most nationwide initiatives focusing on public health,   23._____
        such as Healthy People 2000, place the highest priority on

    A.   alcohol and other drugs
    B.   nutrition
    C.   maternal and infant health
    D.   food and drug safety

24. Problems or shortcomings associated with the client-centered approach to health educa-   24.____
tion include:
   I. Clients tend to overemphasize environmental determinants of health, such as socio-economic conditions and unemployment.
   II. Clients' prior experience may have led them to need and want professional leadership.
   III. Choices of materials and methods usually involve some sort of value judgement on the part of the health educator.
   IV. There may be a conflict between the identified concerns of a client and those of the professional.

  A. I and II
  B. II and IV
  C. III only
  D. I, II, III and IV

25. In conducting a community assessment, advantages associated with focus group inter-   25.____
views include
   I. potential use as a marketing tool
   II. teaching and learning taking place on many levels
   III. possible function as support group for some members
   IV. increased likelihood of candid, unbiased assessments

  A. In only
  B. I, II and III
  C. II and IV
  D. I, II, III and IV

KEY (CORRECT ANSWERS)

1. C		11. D	
2. A		12. A	
3. D		13. B	
4. A		14. D	
5. B		15. C	
6. C		16. D	
7. C		17. B	
8. A		18. D	
9. A		19. C	
10. B		20. A	

21. C
22. C
23. B
24. B
25. B

TEST 3

DIRECTIONS: Each question or incomplete statement is followed by several suggested answers or completions. Select the one the BEST answers the question or completes the statement. *PRINT THE LETTER OF THE CORRECT ANSWER IN THE SPACE AT THE RIGHT.*

1. From a health education perspective, the key to developing strategies for risk reduction in a community is/are the

    A. receptiveness of the community to intervention
    B. particular health risks generally associated with the community
    C. geographic and hygienic factors in the community
    D. shared values and institutions of the community

    1.____

2. As a funding source for health education programs, foundations usually

    A. provide annual reports and funding guidelines on request
    B. provide gifts in kind
    C. don't specify what kind of projects will be funded
    D. don't fund projects requesting 100 percent funding

    2.____

3. A health educator who takes a holistic approach to service delivery is probably more likely than traditional practitioners to make use of

    A. existing government structures and programs
    B. translators or community liaisons
    C. secondary health education
    D. natural support systems

    3.____

4. A health agency has composed a 15-second public service announcement to be aired on local television. The agency wants to learn how and whether the announcement stands out among the clutter of other messages broadcast each day. Assuming adequate resources, the best possible pre-test for the PSA would be

    A. self-administered questionnaires
    B. focus groups
    C. theater testing
    D. individual interviews

    4.____

5. At a bare minimum, a comprehensive health promotion program at a major worksite should include each of the following activities, EXCEPT

    A. group weight loss programs
    B. exercise and fitness programs
    C. nutrition counseling
    D. health risk appraisals

    5.____

6. A health educator is in the process of recruiting workers at an automobile manufacturing plant for a wellness program. The educator should know that the most effective way to involve blue-collar workers in a worksite program is to avoid

    6.____

A. one-on-one counseling or guided self-help
B. setting up screening stations where large numbers of employees work in the production area or the lunchroom, for example
C. a reliance on formal classes for reducing specific health risks
D. attempting to make any changes to the worksite itself

7. In sociology, the _____ theory suggests that society tends toward conservatism and maintenance of the status quo.　　　　　　7.___

A. exchange
B. conflict
C. innovation-diffusion
D. consensus

8. When evaluating the success of a health education program, an agency should　　8.___

A. coordinate the evaluation effort with all phases of the program and all levels of personnel
B. select the most thorough evaluation possible
C. opt for sophisticated and complex evaluation approaches
D. generally ignore subjective inputs from participants

9. Usually, the most effective and efficient way of overcoming a language barrier between a health educator and a group of clients is to　　9.___

A. learn the client language in order to interact more personably with them
B. train and use bilingual community members for use in programs
C. provide a course in English "survival" skills for clients
D. seek the help of a health care professional who is fluent in the client language

10. A health educator plans to use headings as an organizational tool in her food safety brochure. Which of the following statements about the use of headings in printed material is generally FALSE?　　10.___

A. For competent readers, headings are most effective when used with long paragraphs.
B. Visuals with headings allow readers to react before more detailed information is given.
C. One-word headings are more instructional and eye-catching than brief explanatory phrases.
D. Captions or headings should summarize and emphasize important information.

11. Of the following visual tools for instruction or promotion, which is generally LEAST likely to influence behavior change?　　11.___

A. Flipchart
B. Poster
C. Talk board
D. Model

12. In planning a health education program, a group states the goals of its planning process briefly, and then lists in sequence all the steps or activities needed to accomplish the goals. Target data for program implementation is established, and a timetable for each phase of the process is developed. The best way to visually represent this process, in order to illustrate task interde-pendencies, is the

12.____

    A. PERT chart
    B. decision tree
    C. Gantt chart
    D. nomograph

13. Each of the following is an example of primary health education, EXCEPT a course in

13.____

    A. contraception
    B. quitting smoking
    C. personal relationships
    D. nutrition

14. A correlational study reveals a strong positive relationship between the amount of time subjects spend at their workplace and the incidence of obesity. One researcher, studying the data, raises the possibility that a tendency to spend long hours at work and obesity may both be the result of a certain slowing of the metabolic processes. This is known as

14.____

    A. bidirectional causation
    B. a longitudinal relationship
    C. the third-variable problem
    D. a multivariate analysis

15. The main problem or shortcoming associated with the social change approach to health education is the

15.____

    A. assumption that "experts" have the "right" answers to complex health problems
    B. political sensitivity of many health issues
    C. lack of community resources available to many clients to reduce health risks
    D. reliance on the value judgements of the health educator

16. When conducting a survey of the community at large, a health educator should

16.____

    A. select respondents based on their potential gain from proposed programs
    B. collect as large a sample as possible and use these data to make final program decisions
    C. consider it a way of increasing community awareness
    D. combine results with data obtained from community opinion leaders

17. Guidelines for the use of visuals as part of health instruction include

17.____

    I. Images of people in the visuals should look like members of the intended audience
    II. Illustrate both desired and undesired behaviors
    III. Avoid diagrams, graphs, and other complicated visuals
    IV. The number of visuals should be limited to emphasize the most important points

    A. I only
    B. I, III and IV
    C. II and III
    D. I, II, III and IV

18. Which of the following is a risk factor associated with diabetes?   18._____

    A. Drug abuse
    B. Obesity
    C. Environmental factors
    D. Stress

19. Which of the following questions would be MOST likely to appear in the summative eval-   19._____
uation of a health education program?

    A. How often did staff and members meet with local media representatives to encour-
age coverage of the agency's breast-feeding classes?
    B. How many times did the agency submit press releases or letters to the editor?
    C. Which other members of the community besides the local press were notified
regarding the agency's breast-feeding classes?
    D. How many mothers attended the breast-feeding classes that were offered by the
agency?

20. According to the PATCH model of health education planning developed by the Centers   20._____
for Disease Control and Prevention, the FIRST step in implementing a health education
program is

    A. mobilizing the community
    B. choosing health priorities
    C. enhancement of community awareness about the program
    D. developing a comprehensive intervention strategy

21. When making a comparison of mortality rates by race, sex, and age groups, a health   21._____
educator will need to aggregate _____ of data, unless the community is a large

    A. 6 to 12 months
    B. 12 to 18 months
    C. 3 to 5 years
    D. 5 to 10 years

22. A health educator is asked by the agency director to write a public service announce-   22._____
ment to be aired on the radio. The agency has purchased a 20-second spot. The PSA
should be about _____ words in length.

    A. 20-25
    B. 30-35
    C. 40-50
    D. 60-75

23. Professional standards for implementing health education programs at the local level   23._____
include each of the following principles and guidelines, EXCEPT

    A. an emphasis on health outcomes
    B. a fill-in-the-blanks approach to allow communities to establish objectives

C. a focus on professional practice standards, rather than programs
D. the importance of negotiating responsibilities between state and local agencies

24. A health educator decides that in conducting a seminar for elderly Asian-American   24.____
    women on the risk factors associated with osteoporosis, she will adopt a permissive
    communication style. A potential disadvantage associated with this decision is that cli-
    ents may

    A. conform to other people's ideas, rather than develop their own
    B. become fearful and reluctant to take independent action
    C. lose self-respect and motivation to change
    D. not receive important advice or information unless they ask for it

25. As a mass media channel for the communication of a health-related message or public   25.____
    service announcement, newspapers

    A. are most likely to reach audiences who do not typically use the health care system
    B. can be used to more specifically target segments of the public
    C. involve strict government regulation concerning the content of public service mes-
        sages
    D. usually involve the most thorough coverage, but the smallest likelihood of audience
        attention

KEY (CORRECT ANSWERS)

1.	D		11.	B
2.	A		12.	A
3.	D		13.	B
4.	C		14.	C
5.	A		15.	B
6.	C		16.	C
7.	D		17.	B
8.	A		18.	B
9.	B		19.	D
10.	C		20.	A

21.	C
22.	C
23.	C
24.	D
25.	D

EXAMINATION SECTION
TEST 1

DIRECTIONS: Each question or incomplete statement is followed by several suggested answers or completions. Select the one that BEST answers the question or completes the statement. *PRINT THE LETTER OF THE CORRECT ANSWER IN THE SPACE AT THE RIGHT.*

1. Multiphasic screening, now adopted by many health departments, is BEST defined as a   1.____

    A.   new method of testing vision
    B.   case finding procedure combining tests for several diseases
    C.   combined vision and hearing test
    D.   new method of cancer detection

2. Of the following statements that a nurse might make to a patient ill with cancer who says,   2.____
I don't think I'll ever get better. When the pain comes, I'm afraid I'll die before anyone gets here, the one which would be MOST appropriate is:

    A.   I wouldn't worry about that. People do not die because of pain.
    B.   Of course you'll get better. You look much better than you did the last time I was here.
    C.   You should try to have someone here with you and not be alone. Then you won't be afraid.
    D.   I think I understand how you feel, but why do you think you won't get better?

3. In an epidemiological study of a disease, the one of the following steps which would usu-   3.____
ally NOT be included is

    A.   collecting and compiling data on the incidence, prevalence, and trends of the disease
    B.   reviewing the *natural history* of the disease
    C.   making a sociological study of the community in which the disease is prevalent
    D.   defining gaps in knowledge and developing hypotheses on which to base further investigation

4. Adequate lighting in the school is an important part of the sight conservation program.   4.____
The school nurse familiar with standards for classroom lighting should know that the RECOMMENDED illumination on each desk for ordinary classroom work is _____ candles.

    A. 20-foot   B. 35-foot   C. 50-foot   D. 75-foot

5. The relation of fluorine to dental health has been the subject of extensive study for many   5.____
years.
Of the following statements concerning the relation of fluorine to dental caries, the one which is CORRECT is that

    A.   mass medication by fluorine is now accepted as the best means of treating and curing dental caries
    B.   fluoridation of water supplies, though effective, is too expensive for wide usage
    C.   fluoridation is effective only in children born in areas in which fluoridation exists
    D.   fluoridation prevents dental caries but does not treat or cure it

6. There are measures which are effective in the prevention of diabetes in those with an hereditary disposition.
Of the following, the one which has the GREATEST value as a preventive measure is

   A. preventing acute infection
   B. preventing obesity
   C. avoidance of emotional stress
   D. avoidance of marriage with a known diabetic

7. The basis of a program of *natural childbirth* is to

   A. prevent or dispel fear through education in the physiology of pregnancy
   B. reduce premature births and the complications of pregnancy
   C. reduce the maternal and neonatal mortality rates
   D. prepare the mother's body for the muscular activity of delivery

8. The one of the following statements which is CORRECT concerning retrolental fibropla-sia is that it is a

   A. blood dyscrasia
   B. condition occurring in Rh negative infants whose mothers are Rh positive
   C. condition causing blindness in premature infants
   D. complication of congenital syphilis

9. Of the following factors, the one which is MOST important in maintaining optimum health in the older age group is

   A. regular medical supervision for early recognition and treatment of minor symptoms
   B. economic independence which gives a feeling of security
   C. avoidance of all emotional tensions
   D. adjustment of the environment to prevent physical and mental strain

10. The MOST outstanding result of antibiotic therapy in the treatment of syphilis has been to

   A. reduce the toxic effect of treatment
   B. shorten the treatment period
   C. prevent a relapse
   D. prevent late complications

11. To achieve the most effective and economical case finding for tuberculosis, mass exami-nations should be conducted PRIMARILY for

   A. infants under one year   B. industrial workers
   C. elementary school students   D. pre-school age group

12. Though tuberculosis occurs in all age groups, there is a certain period of life when indi-viduals have the greatest resistance to the infection.
That period is

   A. under one year of age
   B. between 3 years and puberty
   C. between 15 and 35 years of age
   D. between 25 and 40 years of age

13. Drug therapy for tuberculosis has proven to be an important tool in the control of the disease in its active stage.
Of the following, the one which has had the MOST satisfactory results to date in that fewer patients develop resistance to the drug and the incidence of drug toxicity is reduced is

13.____

    A.   para-amino-salicylic acid (P.A.S.) in combination with streptomycin
    B.   dihydro-streptomycin
    C.   streptomycin in combination with promine
    D.   penicillin

14. Studies have indicated that the use of streptomycin in the treatment of tuberculosis has GREATEST value in

14.____

    A.   recently developed pneumonic or exudative lesions
    B.   long standing infections which have been resistant to other therapies
    C.   military T.B.
    D.   meningeal T.B.

15. The PARTICULAR effectiveness of chemotherapeutic agents in the treatment of pulmonary tuberculosis is that they

15.____

    A.   are important adjuncts to surgery
    B.   inhibit the growth of the bacillus
    C.   heal lesions rapidly
    D.   render the patient non-infectious

KEY (CORRECT ANSWERS)

1.	B		6.	B
2.	D		7.	A
3.	C		8.	C
4.	A		9.	A
5.	D		10.	B

11.	B
12.	B
13.	A
14.	A
15.	B

TEST 2

DIRECTIONS: Each question or incomplete statement is followed by several suggested answers or completions. Select the one that BEST answers the question or completes the statement. *PRINT THE LETTER OF THE CORRECT ANSWER IN THE SPACE AT THE RIGHT.*

1. The CHIEF shortcoming of chemotherapeutic agents in the treatment of pulmonary tuberculosis is

    A. their prohibitive cost in any long-term treatment
    B. the toxic effects which follow their use
    C. that their use is limited to early cases
    D. the development of bacterial resistance by the host

1.___

2. Though precise knowledge concerning the optimum duration of chemotherapy in treating pulmonary tuberculosis is lacking, the present APPROVED practice is

    A. continued uninterrupted treatment until the sputum is negative
    B. short courses of treatment with rest periods in between
    C. continued treatment for a minimum of 12 months
    D. continued treatment for one year after a negative sputum and cultures are obtained

2.___

3. A community program for the control of tuberculosis must include school children and school personnel if it is to be a success.
Of the following statements, the one which BEST represents expert opinion on the use of B.C.G. vaccine in the school program for tuberculosis control is that

    A. through immunization of all school children it serves as an important control measure
    B. its chief value is that it is an inexpensive and rapid method of case finding
    C. it would nullify the subsequent use of the tuberculin test which is the best case finding method for schools
    D. it is a valuable diagnostic method which would reduce the evidence of contact with active cases

3.___

4. Nutritional deficiencies are a common problem in geriatrics.
The dietary adjustment usually necessary to maintain PROPER nutrition for the average person in the older age group is

    A. increased proteins and vitamins
    B. elimination of fats
    C. increased carbohydrates
    D. elimination of roughage

4.___

5. The death rate from cancer can be reduced by early diagnosis and treatment. It is important, therefore, for the nurse to assist in case finding.
She should know that, of the following sites, the one which the GREATEST incidence of cancer in women occurs is the

    A. mouth   B. skin   C. breast   D. rectum

5.___

6. Many cancers appear to develop when pre-existing abnormal conditions and changes in the tissue are present.
Of the following, the one which is at present considered PRECANCEROUS is

   A. fibroid tumor   B. chronic cervicitis
   C. fat tissue tumor   D. sebaceous cyst

6.____

7. The diagnosis of cancer by examination of isolated cells in body secretions is known as

   A. biopsy   B. aspiration technique
   C. histological diagnosis   D. Papanicolaou smear

7.____

8. Of the following statements concerning our present knowledge of the etiology of human cancer, the one which is TRUE is that

   A. there is definite evidence that some cancers are caused by a virus
   B. some types of cancer are definitely contagious
   C. there is a strong possibility that cancer is transmitted from mother to baby in utero
   D. so many factors are involved that the discovery of a single cause is unlikely

8.____

9. The National Venereal Disease Control Program carried on by the Public Health Service of the U.S. Government is concerned PRIMARILY with

   A. promoting medical programs to provide early effective treatment of infected individ-uals
   B. a national program of education in the prevention of venereal diseases
   C. distribution of free drugs to physicians for the treatment of venereal disease
   D. providing funds for the education of physicians and nurses in the treatment and care of venereal disease

9.____

10. Of the following, the one which is of GREATEST importance in the prevention of poliomy-elitis is to

   A. build up resistance with proper diet
   B. keep away from crowds during periods when the disease is prevalent
   C. immunize with gamma globulin
   D. adopt general public health measures for the protection of food and water

10.____

11. Of the following statements concerning the present status of chemotherapy in the treat-ment of cancer, the one which is TRUE is:

   A. Results to date indicate it may soon surpass radiation and surgery as an effective cure
   B. It has not proven effective except in cases where early diagnosis was made
   C. It must be used in conjunction with radiation or surgery
   D. It inhibits the growth of certain types of cancer and prolongs life but is not effective as a cure

11.____

12. The W.H.O. Regional Organization for Europe has set up a long-term plan for European health needs.
Of the following activities, the one which is NOT planned as a major activity is

12.____

A. coordinating health policies in European countries
B. promoting improved service through demonstration of an ideal health program in one country
C. promoting professional and technical education for health workers in the member countries
D. providing for exchange of services among member nations

13. A health problem becomes the concern of public health authorities when the incidence is great and the mortality rate high.
In terms of this statement, of the following problems, the one which should be a PRIMARY concern is

13.____

A. venereal diseases in young adults
B. tuberculosis
C. tropical diseases among ex-servicemen and their families
D. degenerative diseases of middle and later life

14. Of the following, the one which is now considered to be the MOST common mode of transmission of poliomyelitis is

14.____

A. infected insects
C. personal contact
B. contaminated water
D. infected food

15. The incubation period for infantile paralysis is

15.____

A. usually 7 to 14 days, but may vary from 3 to 35 days
B. not known
C. one week
D. usually 48 hours, but may vary from 1 to 7 days

KEY (CORRECT ANSWERS)

1.	D		6.	B
2.	C		7.	D
3.	C		8.	D
4.	A		9.	A
5.	C		10.	B

11.	D
12.	B
13.	D
14.	C
15.	A

EXAMINATION SECTION
TEST 1

DIRECTIONS: Each question or incomplete statement is followed by several suggested answers or completions. Select the one that BEST answers the question or completes the statement. *PRINT THE LETTER OF THE CORRECT ANSWER IN THE SPACE AT THE RIGHT.*

1. _____ accounts for the LARGEST percentage of personal health care expenditures in the United States.   1._____
    A. Physician services   B. Hospital care
    C. Nursing homes   D. Drug and medical supplies
    E. Dentist services

2. MOST health care expenses in the United States are paid by   2._____
    A government programs   B. Medicare
    B. Medicaid   D. private health insurance
    E. out-of-pocket payments

3. A physician is NOT legally required to report   3._____
    A. births and deaths
    B. suspected child abuse
    C. gunshot wounds
    D. a child with croup
    E. a child with shigella dysentery

4. Diseases more likely to occur in blacks than whites include all of the following EXCEPT   4._____
    A. thalassemia   B. sickle cell disease
    C. sarcoidosis   D. tuberculosis
    E. hypertension

5. Among the United States population, what malignant tumor has the greatest incidence?   5._____
    A. Breast   B. Prostate
    C. Lung   D. Colon
    E. Stomach

6. The MOST frequent cause of chronic obstructive pulmonary disease is   6._____

    A. frequent upper respiratory infection
    B. smoking
    C. family member with asthma
    D. drug abuse
    E. infantile paralysis

7. The ultimate legal responsibility for quality of medical care provided in the hospital rests upon the   7._____
    A. hospital administrator
    B. chief of nursing staff
    C. director of the hospital
    D. principal nurse
    E. patient's physician

8. Routine screening for diabetes is recommended for all patients EXCEPT those with   8.____
    A. family history of diabetes
    B. glucose abnormalities associated with pregnancy
    C. marked obesity
    D. an episode of hypoglycemia as a newborn
    E. physical abnormality, such as circulatory dysfunction and frank vascular impairment

9. Low maternal AFP level is associated with   9.____
    A. spina bifida   B. Down syndrome
    C. meningocele   D. hypothyroidism
    E. Niemann Pick disease

10. All of the following are skin disorders EXCEPT   10.____
    A. psoriasis   B. eczema
    C. scleroderma   D. gout
    E. shingles

11. All of the following are true statements regarding osteoporosis EXCEPT: 11.____

    A. The reduction of bone mass in osteoporosis causes the bone to be susceptible to fracture.
    B. Bone loss occurs with advancing age in both men and women.
    C. In developing countries, high parity has been associated with decreased bone mass and increased risk of fracture.
    D. Thin women are at higher risk than obese women.
    E. Daughters of women with osteoporosis tend to have lower bone mass than other women of their age.

12. The MOST common type of occupational disease is   12.____
    A. hearing loss   B. dermatitis
    B. pneumoconiosis   D. pulmonary fibrosis
    E. none of the above

13. The incidence of Down syndrome in the United States is about 1 in ____ births.   13.____

    A. 700   B. 1200   C. 1500   D. 2000   E. 10000

14. Lyme disease and Rocky Mountain spotted fever CANNOT be prevented by   14.____
    A. door and window screen use
    B. hand washing
    C. wearing protective clothing
    D. using insect repellent
    E. immediate tick removal

15. Individuals with egg allergies can be safely administered all of the following vaccines EXCEPT   15.____
    A. MMR (Measles-Mumps-Rubella)
    B. hepatitis B
    C. influenza
    D. DTaP (Diphtheria-Tetanus-Whooping Cough)
    E. none of the above

16. Lifetime prevalence of cocaine use is HIGHER among   16.____
    A. Hispanics   B. blacks   C. whites   D. Asians
    E. none of the above

17. The effectiveness of preventive measures against chronic illness is BEST determined   17._____
   from trends in
   A. incidence   B. mortality   C. prevalence   D. frequency of complication
   E. all of the above

18. Primary prevention of congenital heart disease includes all of the following established   18._____
   measures EXCEPT:
   A. Genetic counseling of potential parents and families with congenital heart disease
   B. Avoidance of exposure to viral diseases during pregnancy
   C. Avoidance of all vaccines to all children which eliminate the reservoir of infection
   D. Avoidance of radiation during pregnancy
   E. Avoidance of exposure during first trimester of pregnancy to gas fumes, air pollution,
      cigarettes, alcohol

19. All of the following are true statements regarding genetic factors associated with   19._____
   congenital heart disease EXCEPT:
   A. The offspring of a parent with a congenital heart disease has a malformation rate
      ranging from 1.4% to 16.1%.
   B. Identical twins are both affected 25 to 30% of the time.
   C. Single gene disorder accounts for less than 1% of all cardiac congenital anomalies.
   D. Environment does not play a role in cardiac anomalies
   E. Other finding of familial aggregation suggests polygenic factors.

20. MOST likely inadequately supplied in strict vegetarian adults is   20._____
   A. vitamin A   B. thiamin   C. vitamin B_{12} D. niacin   E. protein

21. The MOST common reservoir of acquired immune deficiency syndrome is   21._____

   A. humans   B. mosquitoes   C. cats   D. dogs   E. monkeys

22. A definitive indicator of active tuberculosis is   22._____
   A. chronic persistent cough
   B. positive PPD
   C. night sweats
   D. positive sputum test
   E. hilar adenopathy on chest x-ray

23. Which of the following is NOT a risk factor for development of colorectal carcinoma?   23._____
   A. Familial polyposis coli   B. Furcot's syndrome
   C. High fiber diet   D. Increased dietary fat
   E. Villous polyps

24. According to the American Cancer Society, starting at the age of 50, men and women at   24._____
   average risk for developing colorectal cancer should follow which of the following
   screening regimens?
   A. Colonoscopy every ten years
   B. Flexible sigmoidoscopy every two years
   C. Double-contrast barium enema every two years
   D. CT colonography (virtual colonoscopy) every year
   E. None of the above

25. The MOST common malignancy among women is of the   25._____
   A. lung   B. breast   C. ovary   D. rectum   E. vagina

_____

KEY (CORRECT ANSWERS)

1.	B	11.	C
2.	D	12.	A
3.	D	13.	A
4.	A	14.	B
5.	D	15.	C
6.	B	16.	C
7.	E	17.	C
8.	D	18.	C
9.	B	19.	D
10.	D	20.	C

21. A
22. D
23. C
24. A
25. B
_____

TEST 2

DIRECTIONS: Each question or incomplete statement is followed by several suggested answers or completions. Select the one that BEST answers the question or completes the statement. *PRINT THE LETTER OF THE CORRECT ANSWER IN THE SPACE AT THE RIGHT.*

1. The MOST common cause of death due to malignancy among females in the United States is from   1._____

    A. lung cancer   B. ovarian cancer
    C. skin cancer   D. colon and rectum cancer
    B. leukemia

2. Medicare provides health coverage to people   2._____
    A. under 20 years of age
    B. who work of all ages
    C. greater than 65 years of age and end-stage renal dialysis patients
    D. under five years of age who require long-term hospitalization
    E. who need out-patient care only

3. Insurance approaches to contain cost include managed care plans.   3._____
A popular managed care approach has been
    A. Medicare
    B. Medicaid
    C. HMO's
    D. institutional reimbursement
    E. none of the above

4. The occupational exposure that may lead to chronic interstitial pulmonary disease is   4._____
    A. silicosis   B. pneumoconiosis
    C. asbestosis   D. farmer's lung
    E. all of the above

5. The principal mode of transmission of hepatitis A virus is   5._____
    A. blood transfusion   B. droplet nuclei
    C. fecal and oral route   D. mosquitoes
    E. deer flies

6. The leading cause of death among diabetics after 20 years of diabetes is by   6._____
    A. infection
    B. cerebrovascular accident
    C. renal and cardiovascular disease
    D. diabetic ketoacidosis
    E. malignancy

7. A breast-fed infant may require a supplementation of vitamin   7._____
    A. E   B. B_{12} C. K   D. D   E. A

8. The MOST common organism associated with chronic active gastritis is   8._____
    A. salmonella   B. shigella
    C. campylobacter pylori   D. staphylococcus
    E. rota virus

43

9. The large proportion of tuberculosis in older persons is due to   9.____
    A. recent exposure to tuberculosis
    B. reactivation of latent infection
    C. malnutrition
    D. immunosuppression
    E. substance abuse

10. The leading vector-borne disease in the United States is   10.____
    A. lyme disease
    B. Rocky Mountain spotted fever
    C. ehrlichiosis
    D. Q fever
    E. yellow fever

11. The malarial species causing the MOST fatal illness is   11.____
    A. P. vivax   B. P. falciparum
    C. P. malariae   D. P. cuale
    E. none of the above

Questions 12-16.

DIRECTIONS: Match the disease in Questions 12 through 16 with the associated animal in Column I.

12. Brucellosis   COLUMN I   12.____

13. Psittacosis   A. Bird   13.____
                                            B. Swine

14. Rabies   C. Rabbit   14.____
                                            D. Skunk

15. Tularemia   E. Cats   15.____

16. Toxoplasmosis   16.____

Questions 17-22.

DIRECTIONS: Match the trade in Questions 17 through 22 with the related occupational cancer in Column I.

17.   Pipefitters   COLUMN I   17._____

18.   Rubber industry workers   A. Carcinoma of the bladder   18._____
                                                                    B. Mesothelioma
19.   Radiologist   C. Hodgkin's disease   19._____
                                                                    D. Leukemia
20.   Woodworkers   E. Brain cancer   20._____
                                                                    F. Carcinoma of nasal cavity

21.   Textile workers   21._____

22.   Chemists   22._____

Questions 23-25.

DIRECTIONS: Match the biostatistical description in Questions 23 through 25 with the related term in Column I.

23.   The presence of an event or characteristic at a   COLUMN I   23._____
         single point in time
                                                                                    A. Incidence
24.   Require a long period of observation   B. Prevalence
                                                                                    C. Cohort study   24._____
25.   The occurrence of an event or characteristic over a
         period of time   25._____

_____

KEY (CORRECT ANSWERS)

1.	A	11.	B
2.	C	12.	B
3.	C	13.	A
4.	E	14.	D
5.	C	15.	C
6.	C	16.	E
7.	D	17.	B
8.	C	18.	A
9.	B	19.	D
10.	A	20.	C

21.	F
22.	E
23.	B
24.	C
25.	A

_____

EXAMINATION SECTION
TEST 1

DIRECTIONS: Each question or incomplete statement is followed by several suggested answers or completions. Select the one that BEST answers the question or completes the statement. *PRINT THE LETTER OF THE CORRECT ANSWER IN THE SPACE AT THE RIGHT.*

1. Which of the following factors contributes MOST to infant mortality?   1____

    A.   Motor vehicle accidents
    B.   Congenital cardiac malformation
    C.   Prematurity
    D.   Acute renal failure
    E.   Pneumonia

2. All of the following statements are true regarding tuberculosis in the United States   2____
    EXCEPT:

    A.   Mortality and morbidity rates increase with age
    B.   Mortality rates are higher for males than females
    C.   The incidence is much higher among the poor than the rich
    D.   In low incidence areas, such as the United States, most tuberculosis is exogenous
    E.   In 2015, the reported incidence of clinical disease in the United States was 3.0/100,000 population

3. Tubercle bacilli CANNOT be destroyed by   3____

    A.   heat   B.   cold
    C.   ultraviolet light   D.   phenol
    E.   tricresol solution

4. The MOST frequent reservoirs for tuberculosis disease are   4____

    A.   badgers   B.   mosquitoes   C.   humans
    D.   cats   E.   deer

5. The LEADING cause of death for people younger than age 65 in the United States is   5____

    A.   heart disease
    B.   cerebrovascular disease
    C.   chronic obstructive pulmonary disease
    D.   diabetes mellitus
    E.   chronic liver disease

6. Cooling towers and air conditioning units serve as breeding grounds for   6____

    A.   staphylococcus aureus
    B.   klebsiella pneumoniae
    C.   streptococcus pneumoniae
    D.   L. pneumophilia
    E.   histoplasma capsulatum

7. Diseases transmitted by mosquitoes, mites, and ticks can be prevented by all of the following precautions EXCEPT

    A. protective clothing
    B. mask and gloves
    C. insect repellents
    D. door and window screens
    E. more than one but not all of the above

7____

8. The PRINCIPAL area of study in injury control is

    A. epidemiology   B. prevention
    C. treatment   D. rehabilitation
    E. all of the above

8____

9. Benzene is MOST likely to be associated with _____ cancer.

    A. blood   B. kidney   C. liver
    D. brain   E. bone

9____

10. A _____ test is used when the patient's wishes can be inferred from his or her known religious, ethical, and/or lifestyle beliefs.

    A. subjective   B. relative
    C. limited objective   D. pure objective
    E. none of the above

10____

11. It is NOT true that standard deviation

    A. is the positive square root of variance
    B. is the most useful measure of dispersion
    C. standardizes extreme values
    D. decreases when the sample size increases
    E. of a small size in a sample causes the sample mean to be close to each individual value

11____

12. The difference between the highest and lowest values in a series is called the

    A. range   B. variance
    C. standard deviation   D. coefficient of variation
    E. none of the above

12____

13. The ratio of the standard deviation of a series to the arithmetic mean of the series is known as the

    A. coefficient of variation   B. range
    C. variance   D. frequency
    E. prevalence

13____

14. In a disease which is usually of acute onset, lasts a couple of weeks, and has a case fatality rate of 75 to 85%, the

    A. prevalence is always higher than that of annual incidence
    B. incidence is always higher than the prevalence
    C. prevalence and annual incidence are always equal
    D. mortality rate will be consistently high in all countries where the disease occurs
    E. none of the above

14____

15. A random sample of 20,000 men is screened for a history of excessive sugar consumption and the presence of diabetes.
This is called a _____ study.

    A. prospective
    B. historical
    C. cross-sectional population
    D. retrospective-prospective
    E. case control retrospective

15_____

16. Five hundred young adults who are known cocaine users are assembled together with a control group. Recognizable psychotics are excluded, and the remainder are followed for 3 years to see whether any psychoses develop in them.
This is a _____ study.

    A. retrospective
    B. case control retrospective
    C. cross-sectional population
    D. cohort
    E. none of the above

16_____

17. The FIRST and most important thing for the epidemiologist to do during the investigation of a patient with a communicable disease is to investigate

    A. the first source of infection
    B. the mode of transmission
    C. how many people have been infected
    D. the accuracy of the diagnosis
    E. preventive control of the disease

17_____

18. The single MOST important measure for the prevention of typhoid fever in a community is

    A. a ceftriaxon prophylaxis for all persons who are exposed to the disease
    B. washing hands
    C. immunization of the high risk population
    D. hospitalization and treatment of all known carriers
    E. water purification

18_____

19. Diseases more likely to occur in women than in men include all of the following EXCEPT

    A. Raynaud's disease
    B. sarcoidosis
    C. gout
    D. systemic lupus erythematosus
    E. secondary hypothyroidism

19_____

20. Over the past 50 years, which of the following chronic conditions has experienced the greatest decline in mortality rate?

    A. Heart disease   B. Stroke
    C. Cancer   D. Pneumonia
    E. Influenza

20_____

21. The population having the HIGHEST frequency of thalassemia is the

    A. Jews   B. Italians   C. Chinese
    D. Japanese   E. Americans

22. Over the past ten years, the majority of individuals who were initially diagnosed with diabetes mellitus were in what age group?

    A. 18-29   B. 30-39
    C. 50-59   D. 70-79
    E. 80-89

23. Of the following, the disease LARGELY confined to people born in temperate climate zones and manifested in early adult life is

    A. diabetes   B. multiple sclerosis
    C. thalassemia   D. hypertension
    E. prostate cancer

24. Hepatitis A has the highest incidence rate in individuals in which age group?

    A. 0-9   B. 10-19   C. 20-29
    D. 30-39   E. 50-59

25. Recurrent episodes of low grade fever and arthralgia FREQUENTLY affect workers in

    A. slaughter houses   B. cotton mills
    C. coal mines   D. hospital laboratories
    E. none of the above

KEY (CORRECT ANSWERS)

1. C   11. C
2. D   12. A
3. B   13. A
4. C   14. B
5. A   15. C

6. D   16. D
7. B   17. D
8. E   18. E
9. A   19. C
10. C   20. B

21. B
22. C
23. B
24. C
25. A

TEST 2

DIRECTIONS: Each question or incomplete statement is followed by several suggested answers or completions. Select the one that BEST answers the question or completes the statement. *PRINT THE LETTER OF THE CORRECT ANSWER IN THE SPACE AT THE RIGHT.*

1. Risk factors for malignancies of the liver and intra-hepatic biliary tract may include all of the following EXCEPT

    A. alpha-1 antitrypsin deficiency
    B. aflatoxin
    C. gentamicin
    D. alcohol
    E. steroids

    1____

2. The parasite associated with an increased risk for developing carcinoma of the biliary tree is

    A. ascaris lumbricoides   B. balantidium coli
    C. cryptoporidium   D. colonorchis sinensis
    E. enterobias vermicular is

    2____

3. Of the following, the immunization that should NOT be given to an individual who has received immune globulin within the previous 3 months is

    A. IPV   B. DTP   C. MMR
    D. HBIG   E. none of the above

    3____

4. Which of the following is the LEADING cause of maternal death among pregnancies with abortive outcomes?

    A. Rubella   B. Ectopic pregnancy
    C. Teratoma   D. Defective germ cell
    E. Herpes simplex II

    4____

5. All of the following are leading causes of maternal mortality in the United States EXCEPT

    A. anesthesia complication
    B. embolism
    C. hypertensive disease of pregnancy
    D. hemorrhage
    E. maternal age between 20 and 30

    5____

6. _____ is NOT a reportable disease.

    A. Pulmonary tuberculosis   B. Mumps
    C. Measles   D. Choriomeningitis
    E. Meningococcal sepsis

    6____

7. The scientific field dealing with the collection, classification, description, analysis, interpretation, and presentation of data is called

    A. distributions   B. statistics
    C. standard deviation   D. median
    E. cohort study

    7____

8. What type of treatment regimen should be administered to an infant born to a mother with active gonorrhea?   8___

   A. Single IM dose of ceftriaxone
   B. Single oral dose of azithromycin
   C. Dual therapy of ceftriaxone and azithromycin
   D. Dual therapy of ceftriaxone and spectinomycin
   E. None of the above

9. A precaution necessary for children in day care who have pneumococcal disease is _____ isolation.   9___

   A. strict   B. contact   C. enteric
   D. respiratory   E. none of the above

10. Children who have ever had a life-threatening allergic reaction to _____ should not get the polio vaccine.   10___

    A. gluten   B. peanuts   C. eggs
    D. antibiotics   E. pollen

11. Stillbirths or perinatal death is a result of _____ % of pregnancies in women with untreated early syphilis.   11___

    A. 5   B. 10   C. 25   D. 40   E. 80

12. Strongyloidiasis is endemic in the tropics and subtropics, including the southern and southwestern United States. The single MOST important control measure is   12___

    A. purification of water
    B. food cooked at a higher temperature
    C. sanitary disposal measure for human waste
    D. mass vaccination of exposed population
    E. detection and treatment of all infected persons

13. In a large population, the mode of transmission MOST difficult to prevent is _____ spread.   13___

    A. vector   B. person to person
    C. airborne   D. droplet
    E. none of the above

14. Of the following, the factor contributing the MOST to infant mortality is   14___

    A. seizures   B. prematurity   C. hypothyroidism
    D. congenital heart disease   E. birth trauma

15. Point prevalence studies tend to have an over-representation of   15___

    A. chronic cases   B. fatal cases   C. short-term cases
    D. healthy persons   E. all of the above

16. The PRIMARY function of the federal government in the Medicaid program is to   16___

    A. set standards
    B. provide services in their own institutions *only*
    C. investigate *only* services rendered
    D. pay for services
    E. pay for nursing care *only*

Questions 17-21.

DIRECTIONS: In Questions 17 through 21, match the numbered description with the appropriate lettered term listed in Column I. Place the letter of the correct answer in the space at the right.

COLUMN I
A. Sensitivity
B. Specificity
C. Screening
D. Median
E. Mode

17. The MOST commonly occurring value in a series of values   17_____

18. The initial examination of an individual whose disease is not yet under medical care   18_____

19. May be calculated in an ongoing longevity study   19_____

20. The ability of a screening test to identify correctly those individuals who truly have the disease   20_____

21. The ability of a test to identify correctly those individuals who truly do not have the disease   21_____

Questions 22-25.

DIRECTIONS: In Questions 22 through 25, match the numbered definition with the appropriate lettered term listed in Column I. Place the letter of the correct answer in the space at the right.

COLUMN I
A. Efficiency
B. Validity
C. Reliability
D. Bias
E. Causality

22. The extent to which a test provides the same result on the same subject on two or more occasions   22_____

23. The extent to which the results of a test agree with the results of another test that is accepted as more accurate or closer to the truth   23_____

24. A systematic error that is unintentionally made   24_____

25. Denotes direct effect   25_____

KEY (CORRECT ANSWERS)

1.	C	11.	D
2.	D	12.	C
3.	C	13.	C
4.	B	14.	B
5.	E	15.	C
6.	D	16.	D
7.	B	17.	E
8.	C	18.	C
9.	E	19.	D
10.	D	20.	A

21.	B
22.	C
23.	B
24.	D
25.	E

EXAMINATION SECTION
TEST 1

DIRECTIONS: Each question or incomplete statement is followed by several suggested answers or completions. Select the one that BEST answers the question or completes the statement. *PRINT THE LETTER OF THE CORRECT ANSWER IN THE SPACE AT THE RIGHT.*

1. The community can influence the spread of disease or the collective health and well-being by

    A. providing barriers to protect from health hazards
    B. organizing ways to combat outbreaks of infection
    C. promoting practices that contribute to individual and community health
    D. all of the above

1._____

2. In community health practice, a *community* is defined PRIMARILY by

    A. skin color
    B. geography and common interest and health problems
    C. age group
    D. ethnic origin

2._____

3. *Health,* as defined by WHO, is a state

    A. in which a person is strong, tough, and fat
    B. in which a person is free from disease
    C. of complete physical, mental, and social well-being and not merely the absence of disease or infirmity
    D. none of the above

3._____

4. The CRITICAL element of community health practice which provides a means of solving problems and exploring new and improved methods of health service is

    A. preventive health service
    B. a health protection agency
    C. research
    D. polydevelopment

4._____

5. A social worker who discovers that a young mother has herself been a victim of child abuse, institutes early treatment for the mother to prevent abuse and foster adequate parenting of her children.
This is an example of

    A. health protection
    B. preventive health service
    C. health promotion
    D. health assessment

5._____

6. The treatment of disorders, focusing on illness and health problems, aims to provide   6.___

    A.   direct service to people with health problems
    B.   indirect service by assisting people with health problems
    C.   development of programs to correct unhealthy conditions
    D.   all of the above

7. Community health nursing does NOT attempt to   7.___

    A.   provide services in the contexts of family and community
    B.   focus on cures, rather than preventive care
    C.   serve clients of all ages
    D.   enhance individual, family, and community group health

8. Community health nursing   8.___

    A.   focuses on populations rather than individuals
    B.   does not collaborate with other disciplines
    C.   provides services only on a community basis
    D.   addresses only primary levels of prevention

9. A nursing student asks you about community health nursing. You would include all of the   9.___
following characteristics EXCEPT:
It

    A.   collaborates with other disciplines
    B.   focuses on preventive rather than curative care
    C.   addresses only tertiary levels of prevention
    D.   does not encourage the client"s active and collaborative participation in health pro-
        motion activities

10. Community health nursing promotes a healthy lifestyle by doing all of the following   10.___
EXCEPT

    A.   providing health education
    B.   demonstrating healthy living skills
    C.   prescribing drugs
    D.   directing health care system efforts to provide the client with health promotion
        options

11. Among the INDIRECT services provided by a community health nurse is: 11.___

    A.   Resource planning and development
    B.   Health counseling for clients having potential or diagnosed disorders
    C.   Health education regarding illness and wellness states
    D.   Care for sick clients, including in-home nursing care

12. Community health nursing provides DIRECT services to ensure assistance for clients   12.___
with health problems, such as

    A.   advocating new community health services
    B.   participating in resource planning and development
    C.   providing in-home nursing care
    D.   developing programs to correct unhealthy community conditions

13. Community health nursing promotes rehabilitation by doing all of the following EXCEPT   13._____

    A. reducing client's disability
    B. occupational and physical therapy
    C. incorporating a group focus such as ostomy clubs, Alcoholics Anonymous, or half-way houses
    D. restoring client's function

14. Primary care services provided by community health nurses do NOT include   14._____

    A. providing health services that are the client's first contact with the health care system during any illness episode
    B. assuming responsibility for a continuum of care
    C. formulating community diagnoses
    D. providing services through the expanded role of nurse practitioner

15. All of the following are elements of community service provided by the community health nurse EXCEPT   15._____

    A. assuming responsibility for continuum of care
    B. formulating community diagnoses
    C. planning services that address community needs
    D. identifying community health problems

16. The one of the following which the American Nurses' Association does NOT define as a basic concept of community health nursing is the provision of   16._____

    A. synthesis of nursing and public health practices
    B. episodic care
    C. services to promote and preserve the health of populations
    D. general and comprehensive care

17. According to the American Nurses' Association, community health nursing focuses on all of the following EXCEPT   17._____

    A. health industry
    B. health promotion
    C. health education
    D. holistic management of client health care

18. Basic concepts of community health nursing, as defined by the American Public Health Association, include all of the following EXCEPT   18._____

    A. synthesizing public health sciences knowledge and professional nursing theories
    B. seeking to improve the health of the entire community
    C. only preventive measures
    D. multidisciplinary teams and programs

19. The FIRST people to recognize the need for trained nurses were the   19._____

    A. Romans   B. Greeks   C. Egyptians   D. Jews

20. The Hebrew hygienic code (c. 1500 B.C.) established a prototype for personal and community sanitation standards, including   20.___

    A.   dietary omissions and food preparation guidelines
    B.   personal cleanliness
    C.   quarantine for individuals with communicable diseases
    D.   all of the above

21. Through the Middle Ages, communicable disease epidemics, including cholera, leprosy, bubonic plague, and smallpox, were caused by   21.___

    A.   poor personal hygiene
    B.   excreta accumulation
    C.   poor housing conditions
    D.   all of the above

22. The voluntary nursing services provided to the poor and sick by charitable agencies during the 19th century were known as _____ nursing.   22.___

    A.   public health   B.   community health
    C.   district   D.   family practice

23. Medicare and Medicaid programs necessitated changes in nursing practice, including   23.___

    A.   establishing home health care agencies as bases for community health nursing practice
    B.   revising and standardizing nursing care procedures
    C.   expanding nursing programs to include physical therapy, occupational therapy, etc.
    D.   all of the above

24. The conceptual model, as used in community health nursing, is NOT a   24.___

    A.   symbolic representation of reality
    B.   schematic representation of some relationships between phenomena
    C.   use of symbols or diagrams to represent an idea
    D.   none of the above

25. Conceptual models used in community health nursing   25.___

    A.   attempt to describe, explain, and sometimes predict the relationship between phenomena
    B.   are composed of abstract and general concepts and propositions
    C.   facilitate communications among nurses, and encourage a unified approach to practice, teaching, and research
    D.   all of the above

—————

KEY (CORRECT ANSWERS)

1.	D		11.	A
2.	B		12.	C
3.	C		13.	B
4.	C		14.	C
5.	D		15.	A
6.	D		16.	B
7.	B		17.	A
8.	A		18.	C
9.	D		19.	B
10.	C		20.	D

21.	D
22.	C
23.	D
24.	D
25.	D

———

TEST 2

DIRECTIONS: Each question or incomplete statement is followed by several suggested
answers or completions. Select the one that BEST answers the question or
completes the statement. *PRINT THE LETTER OF THE CORRECT ANSWER
IN THE SPACE AT THE RIGHT.*

1. A set of interrelated concepts providing a systematic, explanatory and predictive view of   1.___
    a phenomenon is known as a

    A. concept   B. theory
    C. hypothesis   D. rule

2. All of the following are true for a theory EXCEPT that it   2.___

    A. can describe a particular phenomenon
    B. can explain relationships between phenomena
    C. is not logical
    D. can predict the effects of one phenomenon on another and be used to produce a
         desired phenomenon

3. Of the following, the INCORRECT statement regarding the symbolic interactionism the-   3.___
    ory is that it

    A. originated in the works of pragmatist philosophers William James, John Dewey,
         and George Herbert Mead
    B. used to study and conceptualize basic social processes
    C. applied specifically to individual study by nursing and other disciplines
    D. provides a means of understanding human interactive behavior

4. The symbolic interactionism theory   4.___

    A. focuses on how individuals define their situations and on the consequences of their
         actions
    B. emphasizes internal family dynamics
    C. analyzes how role definition and interactions develop and change over time
    D. all of the above

5. Internal family dynamics, emphasized by the symbolic interactionism theory, include all of   5.___
    the following EXCEPT:

    A. an individual's role definition
    B. an individual's interactions with others
    C. perception of the person's role within the family
    D. effect of the individual and family on the community

6. The MOST important community health nursing implication in the symbolic interaction-   6.___
    ism theory is to

    A. work within the client's role definition
    B. assess group dynamics affecting the client
    C. help the client self-assess actions and their consequences
    D. evaluate the client, family or community role definition and its effects on interac-
         tions

7. All of the following are major concepts of the system theory used in community health   7._____
nursing EXCEPT:

   A. Systems are sets of organized components that react to and interact with other
      systems in their environment.
   B. Systems are both open and closed.
   C. A system reacts as a whole; the dysfunction of one system component affects the
      entire system.
   D. Systems employ a feedback cycle of input, throughput, and output.

8. According to the developmental theory used in community health nursing, the family   8._____

   A. is not a social system
   B. is not a task-performing unit
   C. does not have relatively open boundaries
   D. is not continually confronting and dealing with change

9. Regarding the use of the developmental theory in community health nursing, it is   9._____
IMPORTANT to
   I.   use knowledge of developmental tasks when assessing and implementing
        needed community services
   II. observe the family at home to accurately assess the developmental cycle
   III. anticipate family life cycle stages and provide appropriate family guidance in
        community settings
   IV. apply developmental framework to only non-traditional families
The CORRECT answer is:

   A. I, II, III   B. I, III, IV
   C. II, III, IV   D. II, IV

10. The MOST important major concept of the Roy adaptation model used in community   10._____
health nursing is that

   A. people are adaptive systems
   B. stimuli, or input, cause system changes
   C. system changes may be adaptive or maladaptive to the system
   D. two mechanisms control the system: the cognator and the regulator

11. Which of the following modes does NOT affect or implement system adaptation?   11._____

   A. Self-concept   B. Role function
   C. Pathologic   D. Interdependence

12. The Roy Adaptation Model is NOT used   12._____

   A. as a framework for assessing the client and the family in the community environ-
      ment
   B. as a basis for client education and health promotion planning
   C. to develop a comprehensive plan of care by assessing only one adaptive mode
   D. to try to maintain and maximize family modes of adaptation

13. All of the following are accurate characteristics of Rogers' science of unitary man EXCEPT: 13.___

    A. Developed in 1970 by nurse theorist Martha Rogers
    B. Based on behavior model systems
    C. Includes developmental model elements
    D. Based on general systems theory

14. The MAJOR concept of Rogers' science of unitary man is that   14.___

    A. self-care agency refers to a person's ability to perform self-care actions
    B. systems are open or closed
    C. individuals and their environments are viewed as energy fields characterized by wave patterns
    D. the family is a social system

15. Which of the following is a community health nursing implication of Rogers' science of unitary man?   15.___

    A. Individuals and their environments are viewed as energy fields characterized by wave patterns.
    B. Systems have four-dimensionality.
    C. To promote and maintain health, prevent disease, and diagnose and intervene in illnesses.
    D. All of the above.

16. Johnson's behavior systems model   16.___

    A. includes behavioral model subsystems
    B. is based on systems theory
    C. was developed in 1968 by nurse theorist Dorothy Johnson
    D. all of the above

17. Among the major concepts of Johnson's behavior systems model is the idea that the   17.___

    A. entire behavior system has functional requirements of protection, nurturing, and stimulation
    B. systems have four-dimensionality
    C. behavior system contains four subsystems, each of which have seven elements
    D. all of the above

18. All of the following are subsystems of the behavior system EXCEPT   18.___

    A. affiliation   B. achievement
    C. implementation   D. elimination

19. _____ is NOT an element of subsystems.   19.___

    A. Drive or goal   B. Predisposition to act
    C. Action alternatives   D. Ingestion

20. The entire behavior system, including subsystems, has functional requirements of all of the following EXCEPT   20.___

    A. protection   B. aggression
    C. nurturing   D. stimulation

21. Johnson's behavior systems model does NOT attempt to 21._____

    A. promote efficient and effective health-related behavior in human systems
    B. analyze the seven subsystems of a client's behavior as functional or dysfunctional
    C. help the client change ineffective responses to effective responses in the home environment
    D. direct and redirect client system and environmental patterns and organization

22. All of the following are major concepts of Orem's self-care model EXCEPT: 22._____

    A. A self-care deficit occurs when therapeutic self-care demand exceeds self-care agency.
    B. Dependent care agency refers to a person's ability to perform self-care actions.
    C. Systems exhibit patterns and organizations.
    D. Self-care denotes performing personal activities necessary to maintain life, health, and well-being.

23. Which of the following are community health nursing implications of Orem's self-care model? 23._____

    I. Implement nursing systems that are wholly compensatory, partially compensatory, or supportive-educative.
    II. Use these systems to meet the self-care needs of an individual, family, or community until self-care agency is restored.
    III. Examine universal, developmental, and health deviation self-care requisites when assessing community health needs.
    IV. Promote a harmonious interaction between the client and environment.

The CORRECT answer is:

    A. I, II, III   B. I, II, IV
    C. I, III, IV   D. II, III, IV

24. Neuman's systems model 24._____

    A. was developed in 1972 by nurse theorist Betty Neuman
    B. is characterized as an open systems model with two components; stress and stress reaction
    C. is based on Gestalt theory and psychology field theories
    D. all of the above

25. The MOST important concept of Neuman's systems model is that the 25._____

    A. core, or center, of the circles represents those things necessary for life
    B. individual is depicted by concentric circles with impacting stressors
    C. outer circle represents the flexible line of defense against stressors
    D. middle represents the normal line of defense

KEY (CORRECT ANSWERS)

1.	B		11.	C
2.	C		12.	C
3.	B		13.	B
4.	D		14.	C
5.	D		15.	D
6.	D		16.	D
7.	B		17.	A
8.	C		18.	C
9.	A		19.	D
10.	A		20.	B

21.	D
22.	C
23.	A
24.	D
25.	B

———

EXAMINATION SECTION
TEST 1

DIRECTIONS: Each question or incomplete statement is followed by several suggested answers or completions. Select the one that BEST answers the question or completes the statement. *PRINT THE LETTER OF THE CORRECT ANSWER IN THE SPACE AT THE RIGHT.*

1. Immunization reduces the incidence of a disorder by preventing its occurrence. This is an example of _____ prevention.

    A. primary   B. secondary
    C. tertiary   D. passive

1.____

2. Detecting and treating a disease early, which decreases the duration of the disorder and limits disability, is known as

    A. primary prevention   B. secondary prevention
    C. tertiary prevention   D. rehabilitation

2.____

3. All of the following are examples of primary prevention EXCEPT

    A. health promotion
    B. attention to personality development
    C. early diagnosis and prompt treatment
    D. marriage counseling and sex education

3.____

4. Which of the following is an example of secondary prevention?

    A. Rehabilitation   B. Screening surveys
    C. Selective placement   D. Avoidance of allergens

4.____

5. Tertiary prevention, which is limiting disability or restoring function, includes

    A. rehabilitation
    B. use of a shelter colony
    C. work therapy in hospitals
    D. all of the above

5.____

6. Most early epidemiologic investigations focused on

    A. chronic disease
    B. infectious disease
    C. accidents
    D. emotional and mental disorders

6.____

7. Current epidemiologic investigations focus on

    A. infectious disease
    B. chronic diseases such as heart disease, cancer, and strokes
    C. characteristics of normal and well populations
    D. all of the above

7.____

8. Crude mortality rate is defined as the number of deaths within a given time divided by the

8.____

    A.   mean yearly population for the group
    B.   midyear population
    C.   number of births in a given time
    D.   population in a place at the same time

9.   The number of yearly deaths for a specific group divided by the _____ produces the specific mortality rate.   9._____

    A.   midyear population
    B.   number of live births in that same year
    C.   mean yearly population for the group
    D.   population at midpoint of $time_1$ to $time_2$

10.   Maternal mortality rate is defined as the number of deaths from puerperal causes in a year divided by the   10._____

    A.   midyear population
    B.   mean yearly population for the group
    C.   number of live births in that same year
    D.   population in a place at the same time

11.   The number of deaths of children under age 1 in a year divided by the number of live births in that same year is known as _____ mortality rate.   11._____

    A. crude   B. specific   C. maternal   D. infant

12.   Incidence is defined as the number of NEW cases of disease in a place from $time_1$ to $time_2$ divided by the   12._____

    A.   population in a place at the same time
    B.   population at midpoint of $time_1$ to $time_2$
    C.   mean yearly population for the group
    D.   midyear population

13.   The number of cases in a place at a given time divided by the population in that place at the same time is known as   13._____

    A. specificity   B. prevalence
    C. incidence   D. specific mortality rate

14.   All of the following are community health nursing implications of epidemiology EXCEPT the use of epidemiologic   14._____

    A.   data to identify health problems and risk factors
    B.   data to plan programs that meet individual, family, and community health needs
    C.   information to institute treatment
    D.   methods similar to the nursing process when planning community and aggregate care

15.   The MOST important step in health program planning is the _____ phase.   15._____

    A. preplanning   B. assessment
    C. implementation   D. evaluation

16. The MOST important major concept of King's theory of goal attainment is: 16.____

    A. Effective transactions or communication between client and nurse promote satisfaction and, ultimately, goal attainment.

    B. The social subsystem encompasses organization, authority, power, status, and decision making.

    C. Individuals have three subsystems: personal, interpersonal, and social.

    D. Individuals are social, sentient, rational, reactive, perceptive, controlling, purposeful, action-oriented, and time-oriented.

17. The MAJOR concept of Maslow's theory of hierarchy of needs is that 17.____

    A. motives influence behavior

    B. basic needs must be met before higher-level needs

    C. motivation is internal and results from individual feelings and needs

    D. the middle circle represents the normal line of defense

18. All of the following are community health nursing implications of Maslow's theory of hierarchy of needs EXCEPT: 18.____

    A. assess the client and environment to determine the level of hierarchical need

    B. prioritize plan of care to the client's level of need

    C. use Maslow's hierarchy when assessing community needs and developing community services

    D. promote meaningful transactions between the client and the environment

19. The KEY idea of the concept of change theory used in community health nursing is that 19.____

    A. change is constant and inevitable

    B. planned change is conscious, deliberate, and collaborative

    C. the goal of change is improved operation of the human systems

    D. the nurse's role as change agent is based on change theory

20. All of the following are community health nursing implications of change theory EXCEPT 20.____

    A. use change theory for planning changes in organizations

    B. use change theory as a base for effective management

    C. use change theory principles when planning and effecting changes

    D. stop refreezing after a change has occurred

21. It would be INCORRECT to say that leadership 21.____

    A. is a kind of dictatorship

    B. is the process of influencing individual or group activities in relation to a goal

    C. is composed of styles or theories

    D. styles are autocratic, democratic, and laissez-faire

22. The helping relationship 22.____

    A. exists to benefit the client rather than the nurse

    B. involves an explicit mutual agreement that specifies what the relationship will involve

    C. assigns responsibilities to the client and nurse

    D. sets beginning and ending relationship boundaries

23. The community health nurse uses the helping relationship 23.___

    A. for successful interactions with individuals, families, and groups in the community setting
    B. to facilitate primary prevention in the client's home before the illness occurs or before hospitalization is needed
    C. when assisting clients with necessary secondary and tertiary prevention measures
    D. all of the above

24. All of the following are true of the process of contracting EXCEPT that it 24.___

    A. is defined as a systematic method of increasing desirable client behavior
    B. is characterized by continuous and negotiable flexibility based on mutual understanding and trust
    C. is not used in the helping relationship
    D. helps the client develop self-care abilities

25. Contracting is used in community health nursing 25.___

    A. when promoting client self-care in the home or community setting
    B. to improve a client's problem-solving skills
    C. in primary prevention to help a client eliminate a health risk, such as smoking
    D. all of the above

KEY (CORRECT ANSWERS)

1.	A		11.	D
2.	B		12.	B
3.	C		13.	B
4.	B		14.	C
5.	D		15.	B
6.	B		16.	A
7.	D		17.	B
8.	B		18.	D
9.	C		19.	B
10.	C		20.	D

21.	A
22.	A
23.	D
24.	C
25.	D

TEST 2

DIRECTIONS: Each question or incomplete statement is followed by several suggested answers or completions. Select the one that BEST answers the question or completes the statement. *PRINT THE LETTER OF THE CORRECT ANSWER IN THE SPACE AT THE RIGHT.*

1. All of the following are true of quality assurance practices in community health nursing EXCEPT:

   A. Present-day community health nursing quality assurance activities are based on the efforts of early nursing and public health leaders.
   B. Nursing licensure was required in all states by 1923.
   C. Community health nursing practice standards were established in 1985.
   D. Community health nursing practice standards were reviewed in 1986.

   1.____

2. All of the following are true of quality assurance in community health nursing EXCEPT:

   A. Evaluation is the nursing process component that addresses quality assurance.
   B. The audit process is an important tool that helps peer review committees determine the quality of care provided.
   C. Quality assurance uses only the general approach.
   D. None of the above.

   2.____

3. The general approaches to quality assurance in community health nursing include

   A. licensure
   B. accreditation
   C. certification
   D. all of the above

   3.____

4. Specific approaches to quality assurance in community health nursing include

   A. staff and peer reviews
   B. utilization reviews
   C. client satisfaction assessments
   D. all of the above

   4.____

5. The audit process is an important tool of quality assurance that helps peer review committees determine the quality of care provided.
   This process does NOT include

   A. selecting the study topic
   B. explicit quality care criteria
   C. reviewing records to determine if the criteria were met
   D. recommending specific action without a need to review records

   5.____

6. A five-stage process involving clients, providers, and administrators to determine needs and solutions is the

   A. planning, programming, and budgeting system
   B. program planning method
   C. program evaluation review committee
   D. critical path method

   6.____

7. A programming method for large-scale projects that uses concepts of time and events to plan, schedule, and control numerous activities is called the

    A. program evaluation review technique
    B. critical path method
    C. multi-attribute utility technique
    D. program planning method

7.____

8. An outcome-oriented accounting system used by agencies to determine efficient resource allocation is the

    A. planning, programming, and budgeting system
    B. program evaluation review technique
    C. critical path method
    D. program planning method

8.____

9. Audits may

    A. be concurrent
    B. evaluate the quality of ongoing care
    C. be retrospective
    D. all of the above

9.____

10. All of the following statements are true regarding crisis or crisis intervention EXCEPT:

    A. A crisis is a temporary condition, with disequilibrium lasting 4 to 6 weeks.
    B. Reactions to crisis cannot be predicted and cannot be prevented.
    C. Crisis results when an individual's coping process proves ineffective or insufficient, causing severe disorganization.
    D. Crisis evokes psychological and physiological symptoms.

10.____

11. It is NOT true of community health nursing that crisis interventions

    A. focus only on the crisis event and related issues when implementing the nursing process
    B. use a supportive approach to crisis resolution
    C. do not teach problem solving skills
    D. facilitate an open expression of client feelings and emotions as part of the home or community assessment

11.____

12. It would be INCORRECT to say that stress

    A. results from physical or psychological forces that require an individual to alter his coping modes
    B. is directly and indirectly related to many physical and emotional illnesses
    C. is based on an individual's perception of a situation as neutral, benign, or stressful
    D. decreases with age

12.____

13. All of the following are true of the roles and functions of a community health nurse EXCEPT that

    A. he/she incorporates various roles that he/she can use in many settings
    B. roles can never blend or overlap

13.____

C. he/she must be flexible, adapting to client needs and situations
D. underlying all community health nurse roles is letting the client function independently to promote self-reliance

14. The BASIC concept of the care provider role is that   14.____

    A. clients are individuals, families, or groups
    B. the community health nurse is holistic, involving the client's physical, psychological, social, and spiritual needs
    C. care provided is either primary, secondary, or tertiary
    D. the community health nurse provides care to clients across the health continuum

15. A community health nurse provides direct care to sick clients in various settings, assessing client needs and formulating a plan of care that includes   15.____

    A. bathing and range of motion exercises
    B. medication and other treatments
    C. ambulation and environment adaptation
    D. all of the above

16. A community health nurse provides indirect care to sick clients in various settings by   16.____

    A. discussing the illness and care requirements with the client and family members
    B. coordinating nursing care with other health care providers
    C. explaining services available from other community agencies
    D. all of the above

17. All of the following are basic concepts of the health educator role EXCEPT: 17.____

    A. Teaching is the foundation of health education.
    B. Health education lets the client assume more responsibilities for meeting his own health needs.
    C. Health education may involve individuals and families, but not community groups.
    D. The family plays an important role in the client's learning, and that information learned by the client affects the entire family.

18. A role model is someone   18.____

    A. whose behavior is adopted by others
    B. who does not illustrate a specific behavior
    C. whose activities are watched by others
    D. who works in show business

19. All of the following statements about role models are true in community health nursing EXCEPT: 19.____

    A. As a role model, the community health nurse gives each client an opportunity to observe positive health practices.
    B. The community health nurse's actions communicate valuable health information.
    C. Role model is used only in primary prevention.
    D. None of the above.

20. The community health nurse, as a role model, functions to demonstrate positive physical   20.____
and mental health practices such as

    A.   eating nutritious food
    B.   maintaining desirable weight
    C.   arranging time to relax daily
    D.   all of the above

21. In order to be an effective advocate, the community health nurse needs to be able to   21.____

    A.   be assertive and be willing to take risks
    B.   communicate clearly and negotiate thoroughly and convincingly
    C.   identify and tap resources for the client's benefit
    D.   all of the above

22. As an effective advocate, the community health nurse's functions include all of the follow-   22.____
ing EXCEPT to

    A.   communicate with referral agencies to facilitate the client's transition from one
       agency to another
    B.   ignore inadequate or unjust services
    C.   promote client advocacy in all agency activities
    D.   collaborate with health team members

23. It is NOT true of the counselor role of the community health nurse that counseling   23.____

    A.   has the goal of effective problem solving
    B.   is based on a positive and helping relationship
    C.   can involve individuals or families, but not groups
    D.   can be used in primary, secondary, or tertiary prevention

24. All of the following are functions of a community health nurse's role as a counselor   24.____
EXCEPT

    A.   helping a client find a job
    B.   helping the client identify the problem and relevant factors
    C.   providing information, listening objectively, and being supportive, caring, and trust-
       worthy
    D.   helping the client find a workable solution to the problem

25. The community health nurse, as a manager,   25.____

    A.   supervises client care
    B.   coordinates agency and community and plans activities
    C.   supervises ancillary health team members, such as home health aides
    D.   all of the above

———————

KEY (CORRECT ANSWERS)

1.	C	11.	C
2.	C	12.	D
3.	D	13.	B
4.	D	14.	C
5.	D	15.	D
6.	B	16.	D
7.	A	17.	C
8.	A	18.	A
9.	D	19.	C
10.	B	20.	D

21.	D
22.	B
23.	C
24.	A
25.	D

EXAMINATION SECTION
TEST 1

DIRECTIONS: Each question or incomplete statement is followed by several suggested answers or completions. Select the one that BEST answers the question or completes the statement. *PRINT THE LETTER OF THE CORRECT ANSWER IN THE SPACE AT THE RIGHT.*

1. The functions performed by the community for its members include all of the following EXCEPT

    A. producing, distributing, and consuming goods and services
    B. not socializing new members
    C. adapting to changes in the surrounding environment
    D. maintaining social control

1.____

2. A healthy community must meet certain criteria, such as all of the following EXCEPT

    A. commitment by each member to the community
    B. effective communication among community groups
    C. member participation is not necessary in community activities
    D. containment of conflicts

2.____

3. Community health nursing affects a community by

    A. considering the community the target of service each time the community health nurse provides care
    B. realizing that a change in an individual's health affects the health of his community
    C. providing care to individuals, families, or aggregates that affect the entire community
    D. all of the above

3.____

4. Community assessment provides the community health nurse with

    A. information about community members' jobs and educational backgrounds
    B. information that helps her know and understand the community as a target of service
    C. the criminal record of the community
    D. all of the above

4.____

5. The process by which a community health nurse assesses information about a specific individual or family as part of the community is called

    A. familiarization
    B. comprehensive assessment
    C. problem-oriented assessment
    D. individual assessment

5.____

6. All of the following are community *location* assessment areas EXCEPT

    A. environment   B. weather
    C. geography   D. education

6.____

7. Community *population* assessment areas do NOT include 7.___

    A. age and sex
    B. race and ethnic background
    C. housing
    D. employment and unemployment rates

8. Community *social system* assessment areas include all of the following EXCEPT 8.___

    A. political system
    B. birth, death, morbidity, and mortality rates
    C. employment base, such as stores, businesses, and industries
    D. official health agencies and services

9. Which of the following is(are) data sources for community assessment? 9.___

    A. Libraries
    B. Churches
    C. Local government offices
    D. All of the above

10. The practice of assessing data gathered from a representative population sample is known as 10.___

    A. epidemiologic study   B. survey
    C. participant observation   D. none of the above

11. Assessing a functioning social setting during direct or indirect involvement in the setting is called 11.___

    A. descriptive epidemiologic survey
    B. participant observation
    C. survey
    D. data processing

12. Individuals united by birth, marriage, or adoption who reside together are called a _____ family. 12.___

    A. non-traditional   B. traditional
    C. biological   D. non-biological

13. A close family friend, often identified as an aunt or uncle, is defined as _____ family. 13.___

    A. workplace   B. honorary relative
    C. traditional   D. non-traditional

14. A nuclear unit consisting of a mother, father, and children is defined as a _____ family. 14.___

    A. biological   B. non-biological
    C. traditional   D. non-traditional

15. A family is a social system. 15.____
It would be INCORRECT to say that family/families

    A. set and maintain boundaries
    B. exhibit adaptive behavior
    C. members are not interdependent
    D. exhibit goal-oriented behavior

16. A family has a specific configuration, which could be a 16.____

    A. nuclear family with one career
    B. single parent family
    C. commune family
    D. all of the above

17. A family's structural parameters include all of the following EXCEPT 17.____

    A. methods of communicating
    B. relationships with other groups and systems
    C. nuclear dyad
    D. distribution of power and authority

18. A family is a social system which performs all of the following basic functions EXCEPT 18.____

    A. socialization   B. reproduction
    C. personality maintenance   D. none of the above

19. Which of the following functions of the family provides physical necessities, such as food, 19.____
shelter, clothing, and health care?

    A. Security   B. Identity
    C. Family coping   D. Affiliation

20. Family developmental tasks for a family with adolescents do NOT include 20.____

    A. balancing teenage freedom and responsibility
    B. maintaining open communication between parents and children
    C. getting a divorce if conflicts arise between parents
    D. building a foundation for future family stages

21. Family developmental tasks for an aging family include all of the following EXCEPT 21.____

    A. adjusting to retirement
    B. maintaining a satisfactory home life
    C. adjusting to health changes
    D. looking for another job

Questions 22-25.

DIRECTIONS: In Questions 22 through 25, match the numbered definition with the lettered term, listed in the column below, which it BEST describes.

    A.   Host
    B.   Adaptation
    C.   Teaching
    D.   Agent
    E.   Learning

22.   Ability to change in response to a stressor.   22.___

23.   Factor whose presence or absence causes disease.   23.___

24.   Human being that provides an environment for disease.   24.___

25.   Communication process employed to change the learner's behavior.   25.___

_____

KEY (CORRECT ANSWERS)

1.	B		11.	B
2.	C		12.	B
3.	D		13.	B
4.	B		14.	A
5.	A		15.	C
6.	D		16.	D
7.	C		17.	C
8.	B		18.	D
9.	D		19.	A
10.	B		20.	C

21.   D
22.   B
23.   D
24.   A
25.   C

_____

TEST 2

DIRECTIONS: Each question or incomplete statement is followed by several suggested answers or completions. Select the one that BEST answers the question or completes the statement. *PRINT THE LETTER OF THE CORRECT ANSWER IN THE SPACE AT THE RIGHT.*

1. Family developmental tasks for a middle-aged family would include   1.____

   A.   strengthening the marital relationship
   B.   sustaining relationships with parents and children
   C.   cultivating leisure activities
   D.   all of the above

2. The MAIN functions of a community health nurse serving a family include   2.____

   A.   working with the family individually and collectively
   B.   recognizing the validity of family structure variations; demonstrating an awareness of nontraditional families
   C.   emphasizing family strengths
   D.   all of the above

3. All of the following are areas of family health assessment EXCEPT   3.____

   A.   basic information about each family member
   B.   resources available to the family
   C.   work environment
   D.   physical and psychological health of each member

4. All of the following guidelines regarding community health nursing implications of family health assessment are true EXCEPT: 4.____

   A.   Adopt a comprehensive, holistic approach to family health assessment
   B.   Maintaining confidentiality of family information is not important
   C.   Consider the health continuum when assessing the family and make wellness-oriented diagnoses when appropriate
   D.   Summarize strengths and limitations relative to each assessment category

5. The functioning of the family system affects each member. The observation of family _____ is NOT an important factor in the assessment of family functioning.   5.____

   A.   members' developmental stages
   B.   links with the community
   C.   education
   D.   coping

6. Which of the following is a family functioning assessment tool?   6.____

   A.   Ecomap
   B.   Family life chronology
   C.   Home observation for measurement of the environment
   D.   All of the above

7. All of the following are true about the family as a client in community health nursing   7.__
   EXCEPT:

   A. The family is the basic social unit
   B. A family has many definitions, but is limited to the traditional nuclear family in this
      situation
   C. Families change continuously during their life cycles
   D. The health of one family member affects the entire family's health

8. The recording of family interactive processes to assess family functioning is called   8.__

   A. ecomap
   B. family life chronology
   C. family sculpture
   D. family coping estimate

9. A high risk population in a community   9.__

   A. diminishes quality of life for the individual and his family
   B. increases community productivity
   C. diminishes community health care costs
   D. diminishes demands on the health care system for services and appropriate pro-
      grams

10. Health care system components responding to high-risk populations that experience   10.__
    chronic illnesses characterized by acute exacerbations include all of the following
    EXCEPT

    A. ambulatory care facilities
    B. hospitals
    C. schools
    D. rehabilitation centers

11. The main *controllable* risk factors for the leading causes of death in the United States do   11.__
    NOT include

    A. smoking   B. hypercholesterolemia
    C. male sex   D. alcohol

12. Risk factors for cardiovascular disease include   12.__

    A. increasing age   B. male sex
    C. hypertension   D. all of the above

13. The population needs all of the following to prevent and treat cardiovascular disease   13.__
    EXCEPT

    A. detection and screening programs
    B. dietary management
    C. medication management
    D. separation of affected individuals

14. Community health nursing functions in the *primary* prevention of cardiovascular disease do NOT include

    A. teaching cardiac emergency measures
    B. providing family and group education on nutrition and exercise, stress management, and self-care philosophy
    C. exemplifying health promotion practices in one's own life
    D. appraising the community's health for specific cardiovascular needs and problems

14.____

15. All of the following are community health nursing functions in the *secondary* prevention of cardiovascular disease EXCEPT

    A. providing direct care to the client and family during illness episodes
    B. exemplifying health promotion practices in own life
    C. helping client and family adapt positively to the illness
    D. informing client and family about available community resources

15.____

16. It is NOT true that cancer

    A. is the leading cause of death in the United States
    B. occurs in all age groups but incidence increases with age
    C. occurs in men more often than in women
    D. mortality rates are higher for blacks than for whites

16.____

17. Which of the following is NOT among the risk factors associated with cancer?

    A. Genetic background
    B. Chronic exposure to chemical agents
    C. Jewish origin
    D. Prolonged exposure to environmental agents

17.____

18. All of the following are community health nurse functions in the *primary* prevention of cancer EXCEPT

    A. teaching client, family, and community residents how to modify high-risk lifestyles
    B. teaching self-screening techniques
    C. providing another job in place of a job with high risks
    D. developing risk-reducing health promotion programs and resources based on epidemiologic information

18.____

19. It is NOT true of diabetes that

    A. the non-insulin-dependent type is more common than the insulin-dependent type
    B. its prevalence increases with age
    C. it is more prevalent in men than in women
    D. it is more prevalent in blacks than in whites

19.____

20. Chronic obstructive pulmonary disease

    A. is not a major cause of adult disability
    B. occurs more frequently in women than in men
    C. approximately 75% deaths are black males
    D. smoking is the single most common cause

20.____

21. In order to prevent or treat diabetes mellitus, all of the following are needed EXCEPT   21._____
    A. education and resources to promote healthful nutrition and weight control
    B. community resources to screen for diabetes
    C. medication management
    D. financial support to the clients

Questions 22-25.

DIRECTIONS: In Questions 22 through 25, match the numbered definition with the lettered term, listed in the column below, which it BEST describes.

    A. Prevalence
    B. Incidence
    C. Crisis
    D. Aggregate
    E. Risk

22. Rate of newly occurring cases of a disease in a population during a specified period.   22._____

23. Probability of an unfavorable event, such as disease.   23._____

24. Number of existing cases of a disease in a defined population at a given time.   24._____

25. Population group.   25._____

KEY (CORRECT ANSWERS)

1.	D		11.	C
2.	D		12.	D
3.	C		13.	D
4.	B		14.	A
5.	C		15.	B
6.	D		16.	A
7.	B		17.	C
8.	B		18.	C
9.	A		19.	C
10.	C		20.	C

21.	D
22.	B
23.	E
24.	A
25.	D

EXAMINATION SECTION
TEST 1

DIRECTIONS: Each question or incomplete statement is followed by several suggested answers or completions. Select the one that BEST answers the question or completes the statement. *PRINT THE LETTER OF THE CORRECT ANSWER IN THE SPACE AT THE RIGHT.*

1. Which of the following is NOT an advantage to using classroom teachers as outdoor-education staff members?   1.____

    A. Most are trained in educational methodology.
    B. Most are knowledgeable about the outdoors.
    C. They are familiar with the participants from their own classrooms.
    D. They are generally efficient users of instructional time.

2. The MAIN difference between the objectives of an environmental education program and its purposes is that the objectives   2.____

    A. are specific, measurable changes in the participants of a program
    B. are designed to be more far-reaching
    C. are concerned primarily with the internal workings of a program
    D. often vary from program to program

3. Which of the following is NOT considered to be one of the basic components of an ecological system?   3.____

    A. Abiotic substances such as soil, water, and air
    B. Weather patterns
    C. Producers
    D. Decomposers

4. Making informed choices between essential and nonessential goods is an objective associated with the _____ domain of environmental education.   4.____

    A. ecological   B. political
    C. social   D. economic

5. Which of the following represents a lower-level activity in the environmental education hierarchy?   5.____

    A. Problem-solving processes
    B. Analogies
    C. Decision-making
    D. Ecological principles

6. In the United States, the main body of environmental information comes INITIALLY from   6.____

    A. government reports and studies
    B. privately-funded scientific periodicals
    C. the mainstream news media
    D. public-funded radio and television programs

7. Which of the following is normally a characteristic of camp-centered outdoor/environmental education?

    A. Experiences are planned in the classroom and applied in camp.
    B. The program is operated by a classroom teacher with the help of trained resource persons.
    C. Camping experiences are evaluated on their contribution to the work of the classroom.
    D. Experiences are not planned to bring out specific learnings, but valuable concepts are gained through incidental experience.

7.___

8. Which of the following is a concept associated with the economic aspect of environmental education?

    A. Public opinion constitutes a control over the use of conservation practices.
    B. Animal populations are renewable resources.
    C. Individuals tend to select short-term gains at the expense of long-term environmental benefits.
    D. Individual citizens should be stimulated to become involved in the political process.

8.___

9. The standard recommendation for an outdoor-education site's distance from a hospital is no more than _____ miles.

    A. 5-10   B. 15-20   C. 25-30   D. 50

9.___

10. In general, NOT considered to be an experience involved in the process of environmental education is

    A. environmental discovery and inquiry
    B. environmental evaluation and problem identification
    C. planned alteration of the environment
    D. problem-solving in the environment

10.___

11. A PRIMARY difference between the instructional and social living phases of environmental education is that during the instructional phase

    A. student groups are not mixed
    B. staff attempt to shape student attitudes
    C. students are taught to share responsibilities
    D. student progress is not evaluated

11.___

12. According to the conceptual framework for environmental education, _____ exemplifies the *macro* level of ecological analysis.

    A. the classroom or school
    B. political or legal institutions
    C. larger social structures
    D. the family and neighborhood of schools

12.___

13. In order to insure that sleeping arrangements in an outdoor education bunkhouse are both safe and efficient, it is IMPORTANT to arrange beds or sleepers so that

    A. there is a minimum of six feet of space between the sides of the beds
    B. there is at least 60 square feet of usable floor space for each sleeper

13.___

C. their heads are at least six feet apart
D. the bunks are tripled

14. Which of the following is NOT an explanation for why environmental education is usually described as a *human-centered* process? 14._____

    A. Humans are an indivisible part of world dynamics.
    B. All awareness and decision-making associated with education begins in the human mind.
    C. Humans alone have the conscious ability to alter the world's balances.
    D. Humans are generally the most important world species.

15. Which is usually NOT a subcategory of the environment for which measurable objectives are targeted in the early stages of an education program? 15._____

    A. Social   B. Biotic   C. Political   D. Physical

16. Which of the following is an evaluative activity for students that would be classified in the category of problem-solving? 16._____

    A. Compiling complete and accurate information in both written and graphic form
    B. Selecting and completing optional assignments related to the selected topic of study
    C. Identifying and defining issues and problems affecting the total environment
    D. Attempting to work harmoniously with others on a given task

17. Which of the following is a concept associated with the political aspect of environmental education? 17._____

    A. Modern humans affect the structure of their environment.
    B. Pollutants and contaminants are produced by natural and human-made processes.
    C. Humans have psychobiological and biosocial needs.
    D. As population increases, the freedom of individuals to use natural resources decreases.

18. The discipline that environmental education is designed PRIMARILY to influence in all individuals is 18._____

    A. art   B. history   C. living   D. science

19. Which of the following learning processes involves the MOST complex set of skills and behaviors? 19._____

    A. Experimenting   B. Observing
    C. Classifying   D. Inferring

20. In the global model for environmental interaction, humans exert influence on the environment by their output through the 20._____

    A. biosphere   B. ecosphere
    C. technosphere   D. geosphere

21. According to most environmental education models, which of the concepts below would be reserved for the latest stages of the education process?   21.___

   A. Philosophy of human/earth interaction
   B. Environmental sensitivity
   C. Factual knowledge
   D. Problem-solving skills

22. Usually, the BEST method of teaching decision-making skills in outdoor education is(are)   22.___

   A. researching the decisions made by public bodies in the past
   B. self-reliance survival exercises
   C. simulation games and hypothetical issues
   D. case studies

23. Which of these curricular disciplines is the one LEAST likely to be integrated into an environmental education program?   23.___

   A. Social science   B. Mathematics
   C. Humanities   D. Health

24. Which of the following is NOT a method for dealing with population growth that is supported by most recent research?   24.___

   A. Engaging people of all socioeconomic backgrounds in the decision-making process
   B. Concentration of birth control and family planning efforts on minority populations
   C. A program of incentives to adopt available children
   D. Ruling out any and all programs for mandatory sterilization

25. In an environmental education program, the objectives that are MOST easily and accurately measured are   25.___

   A. behavioral   B. attitudinal
   C. emotional   D. social

KEY (CORRECT ANSWERS)

1.	B		11.	A
2.	A		12.	B
3.	B		13.	C
4.	D		14.	D
5.	B		15.	C
6.	A		16.	D
7.	D		17.	D
8.	C		18.	C
9.	B		19.	A
10.	C		20.	C

21.	A
22.	C
23.	B
24.	B
25.	A

TEST 2

DIRECTIONS: Each question or incomplete statement is followed by several suggested answers or completions. Select the one that BEST answers the question or completes the statement. *PRINT THE LETTER OF THE CORRECT ANSWER IN THE SPACE AT THE RIGHT.*

1. The collective term for the concepts and values through which humans recognize their interdependence with the environment, as well as their own responsibilities for maintaining it, is

    A. biotics   B. ecototics   C. ekistics   D. socioties

1.___

2. Which of the following is NOT usually considered to be a guiding concept for outdoor/ environmental education programs?

    A. The majority of young children access the physical universe through abstractions, rather than firsthand experience.
    B. Modern living has increased the need for outdoor/ environmental education.
    C. Outdoor/environmental education is not a separate discipline in itself.
    D. In outdoor/environmental education, learning is controlled by instructors who lead students to discover a set of prescribed educational goals.

2.___

3. Which of the following would be an objective for the discovery-inquiry level of an environmental education program?

    A. Defining an environmental issue or problem
    B. Recognizing the living components of a single ecosystem
    C. Determining alternative solutions to an environmental problem
    D. Identifying opportunities for environmental improvement

3.___

4. In the standard progression of outdoor-education activities, which courses would a program's participants engage in FIRST?

    A. Ecological principles
    B. Investigating environmental habitats
    C. Recognizing land-use problems
    D. Outdoor survival

4.___

5. Most environmental education programs are structured around the belief that environmental problems are caused by

    A. the actions of a limited number of political bodies
    B. the way all civilized humans presently try to meet their personal and social needs
    C. industrial trends that begin primarily in the United States
    D. the geometric increase in the world's human population

5.___

6. Environmental components that provide for human physical needs are related to each of the following characteristics EXCEPT

    A. social well-being and interaction
    B. durability or lastingness
    C. convenience and efficiency
    D. safety and health

6.___

7. Which of the following is an affective component of the human attitude toward nature?   7.____

    A. Concern for the existing parts of natural systems
    B. Awareness of the interrelationship of parts of natural systems
    C. Appreciation of the need for stability in a healthy natural system
    D. Awareness of changes in the structure and function of natural systems

8. The human behavior that would be studied and evaluated at the more advanced stages   8.____
of an environmental education program would USUALLY be

    A. residing   B. working
    C. taking leisure   D. obtaining goods

9. A concept associated with the socio-cultural aspect of environmental education is: 9.____

    A. An organism is the product of its heredity and environment
    B. Humans have a moral responsibility for their environmental decisions
    C. Conservation policies are often the result of group action
    D. Plants are renewable resources

10. In order to meet the accepted standard, a site for outdoor education must have an infir-   10.____
mary that will house at least _____ people for every 100 housed on the site.

    A. 1   B. 3   C. 10   D. 30

11. The *strand* approach to environmental education involves each of the following concepts   11.____
EXCEPT

    A. patterns
    B. continuity and change
    C. interaction and interdependence
    D. manipulation

12. Which of the following would be an objective for the problem-solving level of an environ-   12.____
mental education program?

    A. Evaluating the satisfaction of human needs by environmental processes
    B. Recognizing the structure of a natural ecosystem
    C. Determining alternative solutions to an environmental dilemma
    D. Investigating the natural cycles or processes of an individual ecosystem

13. Which of the events below would be MOST likely to take place in the social living phase   13.____
of the environmental teaching progression?

    A. Courses in naturecraft
    B. Discovery activities such as nature walks
    C. Group courses in natural resource study areas
    D. Student preparation of morning meals

14. The ULTIMATE aim of most environmental education programs is to   14.____

    A. stimulate participants' interest and performance in scientific academic disciplines
    B. change attitudes and behavior patterns among its participants
    C. provide a constructive and instructive recreational outlet for its participants
    D. stimulate environmental awareness and sensitivity

15. In developing a curriculum for environmental education programs, which of the following   15.___
    is NOT considered to be an influential factor?

    A. Transferability
    B. Past experiences of students
    C. Socioeconomic status of students
    D. Economy of time

16. The production of art forms is an objective associated with the _____ conceptual   16.___
    domain of environmental education.

    A. ecological   B. cultural
    C. familial   D. psychological

17. In the standard environmental education hierarchy, which concept would students usu-   17.___
    ally be required to learn FIRST?

    A. Patterns in the use of earth resources are affected by people's lifestyles.
    B. An unchecked increase in human populations will impede the maintenance of envi-
       ronmental quality.
    C. The earth is a closed and limited life-supporting system powered by the sun's
       energy.
    D. Environmental decisions are made by both private individuals and groups, and by
       public bodies or their agents.

18. Which of the following is NORMALLY a characteristic of school-centered outdoor/envi-   18.___
    ronmental education?

    A. The program concentrates on academic classes such as math and English, with
       recreational activities as a supplement to the learning experience.
    B. Camping experiences are not directly connected with classroom work.
    C. A trained staff in outdoor education operates the program with the pupils and
       teachers participating together.
    D. The majority of time is spent outdoors, with students learning how to cook and
       build shelter outdoors.

19. Of the duties listed below, the responsibility of a student who acts as a teaching techni-   19.___
    cian is to

    A. assist students in working together on all tasks
    B. supervise work responsibilities such as cleanup and wood-gathering
    C. coordinate songs and activities at evening campfires
    D. assemble materials and equipment for field study areas

20. According to the conceptual framework for environmental education, which of the follow-   20.___
    ing exemplifies the *micro* level of ecological analysis?

    A. The classroom or school
    B. Political or legal institutions
    C. Larger social structures
    D. The family and neighborhood of schools

21. In the global model for environmental interaction, humans are MOST directly affected by input from the   21.____

    A. biosphere   B. ecosphere
    C. technosphere   D. geosphere

22. Which of the following is a cognitive component of the human attitude toward nature?   22.____

    A. Appreciation of the existing aspects of the natural environment
    B. Concern for the future aspects of the natural environment
    C. Awareness of the structure of a natural ecosystem
    D. Awareness of the human potential for improving the quality of any living system

23. A concept associated with the ecological aspect of environmental education is: 23.____

    A. The nonrenewable resource base is considered to be limited
    B. Natural resources are interdependent and will be affected by the use or misuse of their neighboring resources
    C. More efficient use of some resources is the result of technical and marketing improvements
    D. All living things, including man, are continually evolving

24. Which of the following would be an objective for the evaluation/problem identification level of an environmental education program?   24.____

    A. Investigating the processes in a living ecosystem
    B. Recognizing the total components of a single ecosystem
    C. Evaluating the consequences of possible solutions
    D. Identifying opportunities for environmental maintenance

25. Which of the following is NOT a characteristic of most environmental education programs? A(n)   25.____

    A. interdisciplinary approach to instruction
    B. target population that concentrates on a specific age and level of education
    C. continuous evaluation process
    D. problem-oriented instruction process

KEY (CORRECT ANSWERS)

1.	C		11.	D
2.	D		12.	C
3.	B		13.	D
4.	A		14.	B
5.	B		15.	C
6.	A		16.	D
7.	A		17.	C
8.	D		18.	A
9.	B		19.	D
10.	B		20.	A

21.	A
22.	C
23.	B
24.	D
25.	B

EXAMINATION SECTION
TEST 1

DIRECTIONS: Each question or incomplete statement is followed by several suggested answers or completions. Select the one that BEST answers the question or completes the statement. *PRINT THE LETTER OF THE CORRECT ANSWER IN THE SPACE AT THE RIGHT.*

1. A highly complex compound containing nitrogen essential for building and repairing of body cells and tissue is   1.____

    A. carbohydrates   B. fats   C. proteins
    D. vitamins   E. minerals

2. Which of these is *generally* considered superior to other sources of basic amino acids?   2.____

    A. Fats   B. Green leafy vegetables
    C. Poultry   D. Fruits
    E. Milk, eggs, and meat

3. The building stones for the manufacture of proteins in the body are   3.____

    A. amino acids   B. carbohydrates   C. fats
    D. thyroxin   E. bile

4. A *more highly* concentrated source of energy than either proteins or carbohydrates is   4.____

    A. hemoglobin   B. vitamins   C. sugars
    D. antibodies   E. fats

5. Two minerals related to the health of the bones are _____ and _____.   5.____

    A. calcium; phosphorous   B. copper; zinc
    C. chloride; iodine   D. fluorine; manganese
    E. sodium; iron

6. A condition in which the blood is deficient in either quality or quantity of red blood cells is   6.____

    A. arteriosclerosis   B. goiter
    C. schizophrenia   D. anemia
    E. myxedema

7. The CORRECT percentage of body weight of the adult in regard to water is   7.____

    A. 35%   B. 45%   C. 55%   D. 65%   E. 75%

8. The ability to do *better* physical labor may be achieved as a result of eating a breakfast containing both _____ and carbohydrates.   8.____

    A. vegetables   B. minerals   C. vitamins
    D. fats   E. fruits

9. The CHIEF reason for obesity is   9.____

    A. heredity   B. overeating
    C. glandular   D. psychological
    E. eating proteins only

10. The MOST effective method of determining sensitivity to food allergies is the _____ test.   10.___

    A. elimination   B. patch   C. skin
    D. Minnesota   E. Salmonellosis

11. The MOST sensible way to lose weight is to   11.___

    A. cut out breakfast
    B. cut out the noon meal
    C. cut out the evening meal
    D. discuss losing weight with your physician
    E. drink less water

12. Your activities are the products of the   12.___

    A. nervous system   B. endocrine system
    C. thyroid gland   D. parathyroid gland
    E. gonads

13. The products of the endocrine glands are called   13.___

    A. hormones   B. chromosomes   C. eugenics
    D. pneumococcus   E. toxins

14. Olfactory cells are important to us in regard to   14.___

    A. tasting   B. touching   C. hearing
    D. smelling   E. production

15. The taste buds are imbedded in the   15.___

    A. throat   B. tongue
    C. teeth   D. roof of the mouth
    E. esophagus

16. Excessive amounts of caffein may result in   16.___

    A. indigestion   B. nervousness   C. sleeplessness
    D. irritability   E. all of the above

17. On a camping trip, the BEST way to purify drinking water is to   17.___

    A. boil the water
    B. filter the water
    C. store the water in reservoirs and allow the impurities to settle
    D. chlorinate the water

18. Trichinosis is a disease which may result from eating insufficiently cooked   18.___

    A. veal   B. pork   C. mutton   D. fowl

19. The normal temperature of the human body is _____ degrees.   19.___

    A. 68   B. 90   C. 98.6   D. 99.4

20. The BEST treatment for a cold is to

    A. take a laxative
    B. go to bed
    C. exercise vigorously to work up a sweat
    D. gargle

20.____

21. If sugar is found regularly in the urine, the disease which may be present is

    A. diabetes   B. anthrax   C. rheumatism   D. beriberi

21.____

22. A psychiatrist specializes in the field of

    A. psychology
    B. infectious diseases
    C. high blood pressure and other circulatory diseases
    D. mental or emotional problems

22.____

23. A person with persistent bad breath should

    A. clean his teeth several times daily to kill the odor
    B. have a medical examination to determine the cause
    C. gargle several times daily to kill the odor
    D. chew gum when with other people

23.____

24. The BEST way for students to learn about health is by

    A. listening to their family and friends
    B. personal experience
    C. a study of scientific facts
    D. listening to the radio

24.____

25. Sensitivity to proteins contained in pollen, feathers, etc. may be the cause of

    A. tuberculosis   B. pyorrhea
    C. arthritis   D. hay fever

25.____

26. Identify the FALSE statement.

    A. Ability to drive a car is directly related to maturity and judgment.
    B. It is safe for a good swimmer to swim alone in a regular swimming pool.
    C. A pedestrian should walk on the left side of the road so that he will face the cars coming from the opposite direction.
    D. Carrying a passenger on a bicycle is not a safe practice.

26.____

27. When a person who has been sick is recovering, he is said to be

    A. regenerating   B. anemic
    C. convalescing   D. infectious

27.____

28. The tuberculin test is helpful in determining which

    A. people are immune to tuberculosis
    B. people have been infected with tuberculosis germs and need to be x-rayed
    C. people have recovered from tuberculosis
    D. part of the body is infected

28.____

29. The disease MOST likely to be fatal is

    A. mumps   B. chicken pox
    C. scurvy   D. tetanus (lockjaw)

29.___

30. Identify the TRUE statement regarding the *killing of a fever* by drinking whiskey.

    A. There is neither harm nor value in this method.
    B. The use of whiskey to *kill a fever* is standard medical practice.
    C. It is a little-known method but one that is frequently of value.
    D. It is more dangerous than helpful.

30.___

31. The term *Basic 7* refers to the seven

    A. rules for saving the nutritive value of foods
    B. minerals required by the body
    C. food groups which we need daily
    D. vitamins found in food

31.___

32. Identify the MOST accurate statement about the effect of alcohol on muscular coordination.

    A. An alcoholic drink just before playing a round of golf will increase a player's muscular coordination.
    B. The effect of alcohol on muscular coordination depends *largely* on the health of the individual.
    C. An alcoholic drink just before leaving a party will NOT decrease one's muscular coordination in driving an automobile.
    D. There is considerable evidence that the use of alcohol affects muscular coordination.

32.___

33. If an artery in the lower forearm has been cut, the pressure should be applied

    A. between the cut and the wrist
    B. either at the wrist or the elbow
    C. between the cut and the elbow
    D. both at the wrist and the elbow

33.___

34. Which statement about posture is FALSE?

    A. Poor posture makes one appear less conspicuous.
    B. Carelessness is the cause of MOST poor posture.
    C. Poor posture increases fatigue.
    D. *Stand tall*, *Walk tall*, and *Sit tall* are the chief rules for good posture.

34.___

35. Beriberi, rickets, scurvy, and pellagra are _____ diseases.

    A. circulatory   B. nutritional
    C. communicable   D. occupational

35.___

36. Which statement about nutrition is FALSE?

    A. Most leafy vegetables are rich in vitamins and minerals.
    B. There is no harm in drinking orange juice and milk at the same meal.
    C. Fish is of no special value as a brain food.
    D. Drinking more than six glasses of water daily is fattening.

36.___

37. Another name for poliomyelitis is

    A. tonsilitis   B. goiter
    C. infantile paralysis   D. appendicitis

37.____

38. The mineral needed by red corpuscles in the blood to help them carry oxygen is

    A. iron   B. calcium   C. fluorine   D. phosphorus

38.____

39. Emotional instability in adults is MOST frequently attributed to

    A. heredity   B. heart conditions
    C. head injuries   D. childhood home life

39.____

40. Accidents due to _____ occur MOST often in the home.

    A. falls
    B. poisoning from drugs and cleansing materials
    C. burns and scalds
    D. gas poisoning

40.____

KEY (CORRECT ANSWERS)

1. C	11. D	21. A	31. C
2. E	12. A	22. D	32. D
3. A	13. A	23. B	33. C
4. E	14. D	24. C	34. A
5. A	15. B	25. D	35. B
6. D	16. E	26. B	36. D
7. D	17. A	27. C	37. C
8. D	18. B	28. B	38. A
9. B	19. C	29. D	39. D
10. C	20. B	30. D	40. A

TEST 2

DIRECTIONS: Each question or incomplete statement is followed by several suggested answers or completions. Select the one that BEST answers the question or completes the statement. *PRINT THE LETTER OF THE CORRECT ANSWER IN THE SPACE AT THE RIGHT.*

1. Athlete's foot is caused by   1.____

    A. streptococcus   B. oxides   C. bacillus
    D. fungi   E. streptomycin

2. An adult has _____ permanent teeth.   2.____

    A. 26   B. 28   C. 30   D. 32   E. 36

3. Although some digested foods are absorbed by the blood stream in the stomach, MOST   3.____
    absorption takes place in the

    A. liver   B. pancreas
    C. gall bladder   D. large intestine
    E. small intestine

4. The LARGEST gland in the body is said to be the   4.____

    A. liver   B. brain   C. heart
    D. stomach   E. large intestine

5. Jaundice results from   5.____

    A. excessive amounts of bile being produced
    B. a shortage of lymph
    C. bile ducts being blocked
    D. an improper diet
    E. none of the above

6. When the feces is slowed down in its passage through the colon, a condition of _____ 6.____
    is the result.

    A. diarrhea   B. hemorrhoids   C. indigestion
    D. constipation   E. jaundice

7. Ulcers are *usually* caused by   7.____

    A. irregularities in heart beat
    B. varicose veins
    C. rapid peristalic movement
    D. excessive amounts of acid in the digestive juices
    E. none of the above

8. Sleeping pills *usually* contain   8.____

    A. marijuana   B. cocaine   C. antitoxin
    D. agglutinins   E. hypnotics

9. The Schick test is administered to determine if a person is immune to   9._____

   A. diphtheria   B. scarlet fever   C. typhoid fever
   D. tuberculosis   E. none of the above

10. A vaccine is made up of   10._____

   A. botulism   B. trichinosis
   C. dead or weakened germs   D. anthrax
   E. brucellosis

11. Tuberculosis is caused by a   11._____

   A. virus   B. toxin   C. bacillus
   D. infection   E. toxoid

12. Hydrophobia is   12._____

   A. abnormal desire for water
   B. rabies
   C. abnormal fear of darkness
   D. drowning
   E. fear of heights

13. Poor posture among school-age children is a(n)   13._____

   A. orthopedic defect   B. poliomyelitis defect
   C. osteomyelitis defect   D. epidemiologist defect
   E. none of the above

14. _____ is(are) NOT used for the treatment of cancer.   14._____

   A. X-rays   B. Radium   C. Radioisotopes
   D. Hormones   E. Surgery

15. Hypochrondia describes a person who   15._____

   A. fears the dark   B. daydreams
   C. imagines illnesses   D. fears water
   E. enjoys burning things

16. Alcohol is *one* type of   16._____

   A. tranquilizer   B. pep pill   C. depressant
   D. stimulant   E. all of the above

17. Ophthalmology is a disease of the   17._____

   A. ears   B. nose   C. throat   D. eyes   E. feet

18. A basal metabolism test is taken to determine if   18._____

   A. the heartbeat is normal
   B. the thyroid gland is functioning properly
   C. constipation exists
   D. blood pressure is normal
   E. barbituates exist in the blood

19. The astigmatism test will determine the person's ability to   19.__

    A. see   B. hear   C. write   D. speak   E. reason

20. A skin specialist may also be called a   20.__

    A. chiropodist   B. epidemiologist   C. dermatologist
    D. podiatrist   E. none of the above

21. An electro-cardiograph   21.__

    A. photographs kidneys   B. charts heart beats
    C. records blood pressure   D. records reaction time
    E. photographs lungs

22. Regular vigorous physical exercise will gradually   22.__

    A. increase the number of body muscles
    B. develop good character traits
    C. develop a heart condition
    D. increase heart efficiency
    E. weaken a person

23. Another name for hernia is   23.__

    A. laceration   B. groin
    C. rupture   D. incision

24. The proceeds from the sale of a certain Christmas seal is used to fight   24.__

    A. cancer   B. heart diseases
    C. infantile paralysis   D. tuberculosis

25. The nutrient of _____ is acted upon by bacteria in the mouth to produce acids which   25.__
dissolve tooth enamel.

    A. protein   B. ascorbic acid
    C. sugar   D. phosphorus

26. In the winter, many people place pans of water on the stove or radiator to keep the air in   26.__
the house from becoming too dry.
A MORE feasible and healthful way of keeping the air sufficiently moist is to

    A. keep the room temperature down to 68 or 70 degrees
    B. keep the temperature high - at least up to 80 degrees
    C. open the windows at least twice a day
    D. keep the air circulating with an electric fan

27. An approved first aid treatment would be to   27.__

    A. remove a foreign body from the ear with a matchstick
    B. use a tourniquet to stop bleeding from a minor wound
    C. give salt water and stimulants for heat exhaustion
    D. apply absorbent cotton directly to a burn or scald

28. A blood count of a person suspected of having appendicitis reveals that the number of   28.____
white corpuscles is normal.
It may be concluded that the person

    A. probably has appendicitis
    B. probably does not have appendicitis
    C. is developing no resistance to fight a possible infection
    D. needs a blood transfusion

29. Artificial respiration is NOT applied for   29.____

    A. drowning   B. gas poisoning
    C. corrosive poisoning   D. electric shock

30. The term *enriched,* as applied by the government to bread, means bread made of white   30.____
flour to which has been added

    A. milk, butter, or eggs
    B. iron and thiamine, niacin, and riboflavin
    C. protein, roughage, and fat
    D. calcium, vitamin C, and sugar

31. Fatigue due to sedentary or mental work is *usually* BEST relieved at the end of one's   31.____
working hours by

    A. several cups of coffee
    B. eight hours of sleep
    C. a tepid shower
    D. recreational activity of a physical type

32. Which statement on alcohol and its uses is FALSE?   32.____

    A. Alcoholic beverages are useful in preventing and curing colds.
    B. Alcohol is to be avoided in the treatment of snake or spider bites.
    C. It is a mistake to take an alcoholic drink before going out in bitter cold weather.
    D. Alcohol has limited use as a medicine.

33. Normally, constipation is BEST avoided through the use of   33.____

    A. mineral oil
    B. yeast
    C. laxatives
    D. foods containing roughage

34. In attempting to eradicate tuberculosis, this disease should be considered *primarily* a(n)   34.____

    A. result of faulty nutrition
    B. infection
    C. emotional ailment
    D. hereditary disease

35. Gonorrhea is *frequently* a cause of   35.____

    A. stomach ulcers   B. insanity
    C. baldness   D. sterility

36. One purpose of a periodic health examination is the detection of all of the following diseases EXCEPT   36.___

    A. typhoid fever   B. heart disease
    C. cancer   D. high blood pressure

37. These hormones help to regulate various body functions. _____ is involved when we get excited or angry.   37.___

    A. Thyroxin   B. Adrenalin   C. Insulin   D. Pituitrin

38. To a person driving a car or riding a bicycle, peripheral vision is MOST useful for   38.___

    A. seeing better at night
    B. reading traffic signs more easily
    C. detecting moving objects at the sides
    D. judging more accurately the speed of approaching vehicles

39. Beer, wine, and whiskey should be considered   39.___

    A. foods   B. tonics
    C. stimulants   D. depressants

40. A good substitute for oranges as a source of vitamin C is   40.___

    A. tomatoes   B. beef
    C. cod liver oil   D. whole wheat bread

KEY (CORRECT ANSWERS)

1.	D	11.	C	21.	B	31.	D
2.	D	12.	B	22.	D	32.	A
3.	E	13.	A	23.	C	33.	D
4.	D	14.	D	24.	D	34.	B
5.	C	15.	C	25.	C	35.	D
6.	D	16.	C	26.	A	36.	A
7.	D	17.	D	27.	C	37.	B
8.	E	18.	B	28.	B	38.	C
9.	A	19.	A	29.	C	39.	D
10.	C	20.	C	30.	B	40.	A

TEST 3

DIRECTIONS: Each question or incomplete statement is followed by several suggested answers or completions. Select the one that BEST answers the question or completes the statement. *PRINT THE LETTER OF THE CORRECT ANSWER IN THE SPACE AT THE RIGHT.*

1. Digestion *actually* begins in the

   A. mouth   B. pharynx or throat
   C. trachea   D. stomach
   E. small intestine

   1.____

2. Vomiting is *usually* an indication that there is also a disturbance in some part of the body other than the

   A. stomach   B. mouth   C. throat
   D. small intestine   E. large intestine

   2.____

3. The normal breathing rate per minute for an adult is about

   A. 11 to 13   B. 14 to 16   C. 16 to 18
   D. 19 to 21   E. 21 to 23

   3.____

4. The MOST important to life is

   A. milk   B. meat   C. vegetables
   D. water   E. fruits

   4.____

5. Pneumonia causes an inflammation of the

   A. throat   B. lungs   C. stomach
   D. nose   E. kidneys

   5.____

6. The circulatory system does NOT involve the body's

   A. blood   B. heart   C. lymphatic vessels
   D. spinal cord   E. blood vessels

   6.____

7. To protect the body from infection and disease is the function of

   A. platelets   B. white blood cells
   C. red blood cells   D. hemoglobin
   E. gamma globulin

   7.____

8. _____ carries blood away from the heart.

   A. Venules   B. Veins
   C. Arteries   D. Capillaries
   E. Descending vena cava

   8.____

9. Defects that a person is born with are called

   A. endocarditis   B. congenital   C. cardiac
   D. rheumatic   E. mutations

   9.____

10. The MOST complicated system in the body is the _____ system.

    A. circulatory   B. respiratory   C. nervous
    D. digestive   E. motor

    10.____

11. The autonomic nervous system controls   11.___

    A. voluntary muscles   B. smooth muscle
    C. conditioned reflexes   D. sympathetic movements
    E. involuntary muscles

12. A *spastic* cannot control his   12.___

    A. nerves   B. muscles   C. emotions
    D. environment   E. thoughts

13. The colored portion of the eye is called the   13.___

    A. cornea   B. pupil   C. iris   D. sclera   E. retina

14. Your _____ is NOT one of your body's weapons against germs.   14.___

    A. skin   B. hairs   C. nose
    D. antibodies   E. phagocytes

15. Dizziness and faintness may be associated with a disturbance of the _____ system.   15.___

    A. nervous   B. respiratory   C. circulatory
    D. skeletal   E. none of the above

16. The LARGEST number of people are accidentally killed when   16.___

    A. swimming   B. driving   C. walking
    D. falling   E. flying

17. The LARGEST number of accidents occur   17.___

    A. at home   B. in the water
    C. on the playground   D. at airports
    E. on highways

18. Shock exists because of   18.___

    A. poor circulation of the blood
    B. rapid heart beat
    C. nervous tension
    D. drop in body temperature
    E. open wound

19. A floor burn would be considered a(n) _____ wound.   19.___

    A. incised   B. abrasion   C. laceration
    D. puncture   E. bruise

20. A doctor uses a sphygmomanometer to test   20.___

    A. reaction time
    B. heart beat
    C. pulse rate
    D. blood pressure
    E. amount of sugar in urine

21. Stuttering is *usually* due to   21.____

    A. emotional disturbance
    B. nervous tension
    C. high blood pressure
    D. lack of muscular control
    E. childhood diseases

22. The capacity of the lungs and heart to carry on their tasks during strenuous activity is called   22.____

    A. muscle endurance
    B. muscle tone
    C. cardiorespiratory endurance
    D. respiration

23. A chiropodist is a specialist who treats the   23.____

    A. eyes   B. ears   C. feet   D. nose   E. mouth

24. Malignant tumor is associated with   24.____

    A. tuberculosis   B. heart disease   C. rabies
    D. moles   E. cancer

25. The LARGEST pores of the body are found on the   25.____

    A. arms   B. legs   C. back   D. chest   E. feet

26. The chemical salt of _____, when found in drinking water or applied directly to the teeth, seems to help reduce tooth decay.   26.____

    A. chlorides   B. fluorides   C. sulphates   D. nitrates

27. When cold air or cold water hits the skin, the body reduces heat loss *principally* by   27.____

    A. expanding the pores in the skin
    B. generating more heat in the muscles
    C. reducing the size of the blood vessels in the skin
    D. making the heart beat faster

28. A cup of coffee with sugar but WITHOUT cream contains *only*   28.____

    A. vitamin B   B. calories
    C. protein   D. roughage

29. A deficiency of _____ is a cause of night blindness.   29.____

    A. iodine   B. protein   C. vitamin A   D. vitamin c

30. MOST authorities believe the usual cause of color blindness is that it   30.____

    A. is an inherited characteristic, and so runs in families
    B. may develop from looking at brightly colored lights, especially red ones
    C. is a contagious infection caused by a filterable virus
    D. is caused by an injury to the eyes

31. Active acquired immunity occurs when a person has a disease and then recovers from it. 31.___
This is common for the diseases of _____ and _____.

  A. tuberculosis; malaria
  B. measles; chicken pox
  C. colds; pneumonia
  D. diabetes; anemia

32. It is TRUE that   32.___

  A. raw meat is of no special value in treating a black eye
  B. goiter may be cured by wearing a string of amber beads around the neck, if the beads are kept in constant contact with the enlarged thyroid gland
  C. snake oil will cure rheumatism if the oil is thoroughly rubbed into the affected parts
  D. men whose work is largely mental and who wear hats are more likely to become bald than other men

33. The condition of _____ frequently makes the air less healthful in the home, school, or office during the winter.   33.___

  A. dampness
  B. lack of sufficient oxygen
  C. too much carbon dioxide
  D. room temperature too high

34. Antitoxin pertains to   34.___

  A. immunization
  B. sterilization
  C. germ-killing drugs
  D. determination of susceptibility to a disease

35. When many people in a community have hookworm, it is *likely* that they   35.___

  A. eat poorly cooked pork
  B. go barefooted
  C. have an inadequate diet
  D. do NOT have the doors and windows of their homes screened

36. MOST people who are overweight are so because they   36.___

  A. exercise too little
  B. have inherited a tendency to be overweight
  C. have an underactive thyroid gland
  D. eat too much

37. A meal which consists of bread, macaroni, rice pudding, and cake contains an excess of   37.___

  A. protein
  B. vitamins
  C. carbohydrates
  D. fats

38. Which statement about sunburn is FALSE?   38.___

  A. Sunburn is similar to any other burn and should be treated in the same manner.
  B. If a person who is badly sunburned develops a fever, a doctor should be called.
  C. A severe sunburn may be more serious than other burns of like extent.
  D. There is no danger of getting sunburned on a cloudy day.

39. Goiter may be caused by a lack of _____ in the diet or drinking water.   39.____

  A. iodine   B. chlorine   C. fluorine   D. bromine

40. It is FALSE that   40.____

  A. secondary sex characteristics generally become evident at adolescence
  B. the female reproductive organs which produce eggs are called ovaries
  C. the male reproductive organs which produce sperm are called testes
  D. girls and boys mature on the average at the same age

KEY (CORRECT ANSWERS)

1.	A	11.	E	21.	A	31.	B
2.	A	12.	B	22.	C	32.	A
3.	C	13.	C	23.	C	33.	D
4.	D	14.	C	24.	E	34.	A
5.	B	15.	B	25.	C	35.	B
6.	D	16.	B	26.	B	36.	D
7.	B	17.	A	27.	C	37.	C
8.	C	18.	A	28.	B	38.	D
9.	B	19.	B	29.	C	39.	A
10.	C	20.	D	30.	A	40.	B

TEST 4

DIRECTIONS: Each question or incomplete statement is followed by several suggested answers or completions. Select the one that BEST answers the question or completes the statement. *PRINT THE LETTER OF THE CORRECT ANSWER IN THE SPACE AT THE RIGHT.*

1. A state health officer is *generally* a   1.___

   A. specialist
   B. physician
   C. health educator
   D. member of the bar association
   E. nurse

2. The SEVEREST forms of mental illnesses are classified as   2.___

   A. neurosis   B. psychosis
   C. sublimations   D. personality disorders
   E. peristalsis

3. Security is considered the number one need.   3.___
   It is BEST satisfied by

   A. achieving wealth
   B. attaining social position
   C. being wanted
   D. obtaining maximum physical health
   E. all of the above

4. The appendix   4.___

   A. aids in elimination   B. aids in respiration
   C. serves no function   D. fights bacteria
   E. aids in digestion

5. Diabetes is a disease of the   5.___

   A. pancreas   B. kidney   C. spleen
   D. gonads   E. veins

6. MOST all children are born   6.___

   A. with astigmatism   B. nearsighted
   C. farsighted   D. unable to hear
   E. blind

7. In these modern days, alcoholism is considered a   7.___

   A. habit   B. disease   C. sickness
   D. pleasure   E. weakness

8. Alcohol is absorbed directly from the   8.___

   A. small intestine   B. large intestine   C. stomach
   D. gall bladder   E. kidneys

9. Anesthetics produce

9.____

A. a feeling of warmth   B. diseases
C. a loss of pain   D. freedom from diseases
E. tuberculosis

10. The PRIMARY fault of self-prescribed drugs is that they

10.____

A. are too costly
B. do not cure the cause
C. are hard to get
D. are too slow in acting
E. weaken the taker

11. Disease-producing bacteria form a poison called

11.____

A. pimples   B. toxins   C. inflammation
D. spores   E. bacilli

12. _____ diseases last for a long period of time.

12.____

A. Chronic   B. Cochlea   C. Anaesthetic
D. Analgesic   E. Acute

13. Rocky Mountain spotted fever is spread by

13.____

A. ants   B. dogs   C. feces   D. ticks   E. flies

14. Which word is NOT related to the others?

14.____

A. Antitoxins   B. Antibodies   C. Phagocytes
D. Vaccine   E. Intravenous

15. The MOST frequent cause of death is

15.____

A. cancer   B. nephritis   C. tuberculosis
D. heart disease   E. skin disease

16. A group of similar cells working together is called a(n)

16.____

A. organ   B. tissue   C. nucleus   D. nerve   E. bine

17. The contraction of striated muscle cells is controlled by the

17.____

A. person   B. nerves   C. heart
D. tissues   E. cartilages

18. The muscles are fastened to the bones at both ends by

18.____

A. ligament   B. ossification   C. cartilages
D. tendons   E. coccyx

19. The outer layer of the skin is called the

19.____

A. callus   B. dermis   C. papillae
D. epidermis   E. cuticle

20. Human eggs are produced in the

   A. vagina   B. uterus
   C. ovaries   D. fallopian tube
   E. conceptus

20.___

21. Heredity plays an important part in the transmission of

   A. cancer   B. color blindness   C. heart disease
   D. tuberculosis   E. streptococcus

21.___

22. Fatigue is produced by accumulations of dioxide and lactic acid in

   A. the muscle cells   B. lungs
   C. respiratory system   D. nerve cells
   E. cardiac muscles

22.___

23. _____ is NOT a function of the bones of the body.

   A. Support
   B. Attachment of muscles
   C. Manufacture of blood cells
   D. Protection
   E. Weight

23.___

24. A hernia, or rupture, is more common in

   A. young girls   B. middle-aged women
   C. infants   D. men
   E. older women

24.___

25. The mysterious crippling disease is known as

   A. muscular dystrophy   B. poliomyelitis
   C. tetanus   D. trichinosis
   E. cerebral palsy

25.___

26. An inflamed area containing pus is called

   A. blackhead   B. impetigo   C. pustule
   D. boil   E. fever blister

26.___

27. _____ is(are) the MOST important concerning vitamin D.

   A. Green vegetables   B. Lean meat
   C. Sunshine   D. Butter
   E. Fruits

27.___

28. To recover from tuberculosis, it is MOST important to

   A. rest a great deal
   B. move to a dry climate
   C. exercise by taking long walks
   D. take injections of tuberculin

28.___

29. The cooking of foods decreases their nutritional value in respect to

   A. proteins   B. starch   C. vitamins   D. fats

29.___

30. The _____ destroy disease germs by surrounding and devouring them.　　　　30._____

　　A. red corpuscles　　　　　　　　B. white corpuscles
　　C. blood platelets　　　　　　　　D. interstitial cells

31. An unconscious person should be given _____ as a first aid measure.　　　　31._____

　　A. water　　　　　　　　　　　　B. whiskey or brandy
　　C. coffee or tea　　　　　　　　　D. nothing

32. The scientific name for the female reproductive cell is　　　　32._____

　　A. sperm　　　　B. ovum　　　　C. gamete　　　　D. embryo

33. Little or no roughage is contained in　　　　33._____

　　A. raw fruits　　　　　　　　　　B. whole-grain cereals
　　C. sugar and candy　　　　　　　D. vegetables

34. The term *fracture,* as used in first aid, means a(n)　　　　34._____

　　A. bone out of joint　　　　　　　B. broken bone
　　C. injury to a cartilage　　　　　　D. severed tendon

35. A disease in which certain body cells seem to *grow wild,* thereby destroying the regular　　　35._____
cells and tissues, is

　　A. leprosy　　　　B. ulcers　　　　C. cancer　　　　D. hernia

36. It is NOT advisable to use cathartics and laxatives regularly because they　　　　36._____

　　A. weaken the muscle tone of the intestines
　　B. destroy the enzymes of digestion
　　C. cause one to lose appetite
　　D. cause one to lose weight

37. Diseases which can be transmitted from one person to another by germs are　　　37._____

　　A. infectious　　　　　　　　　　B. hereditary
　　C. allergies　　　　　　　　　　　D. non-communicable

38. Where should a well on a hillside farmyard be drilled?　　　　38._____

　　A. At the bottom of the hill, if the barn, pigpen, and outdoor toilet are on the hill
　　B. On the hillside above the farm buildings and stockyards
　　C. At least 100 feet to the side of the farm buildings and stockyards
　　D. The location is unimportant provided the well is completely covered at all times

39. The soft tissue which underlies the hard outer enamel of a tooth is called　　　39._____

　　A. dentine　　　　　　　　　　　B. cement
　　C. connective tissue　　　　　　　D. root

40. Which statement on the reliability and accuracy of health advertising over the radio is　　　40._____
TRUE?

　　A. It is very reliable since it is censored before being broadcast.
　　B. It may be considered reliable since doctors often prescribe many of the health rem-
　　　edies advertised.

C. Most of it is reliable and can be believed by the public.
D. Much of it is of questionable reliability.

41. The *bends* is a(n)
41.___

   A. gymnastic movement
   B. disease of the intestinal tract
   C. disease of divers and caisson workers
   D. ailment due to inhaling dust

42. The BEST way for a right-handed person to arrange his chair and writing desk in a room with windows on one side *only* is so that _____ the windows.
42.___

   A. he will face
   B. his back will be toward
   C. his right side will be toward
   D. his left side will be toward

43. The blood test required by many states before a marriage license is issued is for the purpose of determining whether or NOT either party has
43.___

   A. hemophilia   B. tuberculosis
   C. gonorrhea   D. syphilis

44. _____ applies to the destruction of bacteria.
44.___

   A. Quarantine   B. Vaccination
   C. Disinfection   D. Inoculation

45. The age period in which lack of proper food results in the MOST harm is
45.___

   A. from birth to 6 years of age
   B. childhood (approximately 6-12 years)
   C. adolescence (approximately 12-18 years)
   D. early maturity (18-24 years)

KEY (CORRECT ANSWERS)

1. C	11. B	21. B	31. D	41. C
2. B	12. A	22. A	32. B	42. D
3. C	13. D	23. E	33. C	43. D
4. C	14. E	24. D	34. B	44. C
5. A	15. D	25. A	35. C	45. A
6. C	16. B	26. C	36. A	
7. B	17. A	27. C	37. A	
8. C	18. D	28. A	38. B	
9. C	19. D	29. C	39. A	
10. B	20. C	30. B	40. D	

EXAMINATION SECTION
TEST 1

DIRECTIONS: Each question or incomplete statement is followed by several suggested answers or completions. Select the one that BEST answers the question or completes the statement. *PRINT THE LETTER OF THE CORRECT ANSWER IN THE SPACE AT THE RIGHT.*

1. During a health lesson, a student who is not paying attention, does not hear the teacher's question. The BEST procedure for the teacher to follow is to

    A.   repeat the question for the student
    B.   have another student repeat the question
    C.   elicit the answer from another student
    D.   reprimand the student and repeat the question

1.____

2. Good class discussion is LEAST encouraged if

    A.   it is guided by questions presented by the teacher
    B.   a give-and-take procedure is employed in evaluating the points introduced by the pupils
    C.   the slower as well as the better student presents his idea even if it may be of little value
    D.   the teacher at the start of the discussion presents his point of view

2.____

3. If a student's answer to a question is so important that it calls for further stress, it is POOR teaching for the teacher to

    A.   ask various members in the class to comment on the answer
    B.   repeat it for its proper emphasis
    C.   follow it with subsidiary queries
    D.   use this answer as the basis for his next question

3.____

4. The MOST worthwhile technique for the teacher to check on whether and how well homework assignments are being done is to

    A.   collect the assignments daily and return them the next day
    B.   walk around the room and examine each student's homework
    C.   have appropriate answers read aloud
    D.   have the first student in each row examine the assignments

4.____

5. A teacher has just presented to the pupils studying the first-aid unit a verbal description of applying a sling to the upper arm. The MOST desirable next step is

    A.   repeating the description together with a demonstration of the action
    B.   referring to a chart which displays a picture of the sling
    C.   questioning various pupils about the steps to be followed in applying a sling
    D.   having the pupils apply the sling

5.____

6. Of the following, the MOST valid reason for using mimeographed sheets for homework assignments for pupils is that

    A.   the chance of pupil error in copying the assignment from the blackboard is reduced
    B.   they make possible more interesting, varied assignments

6.____

C.   if a pupil is absent there is no problem about getting the assignment
D.   it saves the teacher a good deal of time

7.   The FIRST and MOST important step in planning a test is to   7._____

A.   decide what kinds of questions are to be used
B.   define the objectives of instruction
C.   determine how much time is to be allocated for testing
D.   determine the ability levels of the students

8.   If, as the lesson progresses, the teacher of health feels that he will NOT be able to cover   8._____
all of the content included in his lesson plan, he should

A.   eliminate a final summary
B.   halt discussion and write the important notes on the blackboard
C.   conclude the lesson on the following day
D.   discontinue questioning and complete the lesson by lecturing

9.   The MAJOR difference between the developmental lesson and the unit organization is   9._____
that the unit plan

A.   usually lasts from one week to two months
B.   falls entirely within one subject field
C.   is motivated by some item of current events and is introduced by the teacher
D.   is logically organized around a small subdivision of subject matter

10.   The BEST procedure is to have the aim of a health lesson   10._____

A.   stated clearly by the teacher at the outset of the lesson
B.   contain more than is achievable during the lesson
C.   erased from the board after it has been accepted and understood by the class
D.   grow out of the motivation

11.   Of the following, the MOST appropriate summary for a health lesson is the one in which   11._____
the

A.   teacher briefly reviews the highlights of the lesson
B.   students briefly review the highlights of the lesson
C.   students apply to a situation the information learned in the lesson
D.   teacher quizzes the students at the end of the lesson on the information taught in
the lesson

12.   For an effective final summary, the teacher of health should   12._____

A.   have the pupils repeat the facts learned during the lesson
B.   point out the significant facts himself
C.   determine a summary question as the lesson progresses, rather than in advance
of the lesson
D.   seek a recapitulation of the material presented during the lesson

13.   In health teaching, rapid questioning BEST serves the purpose of   13._____

A.   recalling essential facts learned earlier
B.   developing judgment

C. evaluating viewpoints
D. recalling concrete experiences

14. An organized discussion of a definite problem by a selected group of pupils in a health education class is called a 14._____

   A. forum
   C. sociodrama
   B. symposium
   D. debate

15. The BEST method of evaluating the affective outcomes of health education is to utilize 15._____

   A. anecdotal records kept by pupils
   B. frequent short unannounced quizzes
   C. reports to the class by pupils
   D. standardized health tests with national norms

16. The CORRECT statement regarding the construction of a test in health is: 16._____

   A. It is preferable to use one or two long essays rather than many brief essays.
   B. It is good practice to have the list of responses the same in number as the list of premises in a matching question.
   C. The chances of students answering more true-false items correctly on the basis of chance increases as the number of items increases.
   D. It is generally agreed that test items should be arranged in order of difficulty going from easy items and gradually progressing to more difficult ones.

17. In the planning of developmental lessons there should be great *similarity* of the 17._____

   A. aim and motivation
   B. motivation and medical summary
   C. aim and summary
   D. pivotal questions and summary

18. The BEST approach for determining content, concepts, and learning experiences for a unit in health teaching is 18._____

   A. pretesting, surveying local needs and planning by teacher and learner
   B. distributing visual aids and planning guideline
   C. using independent study, motivational techniques and socio-drama
   D. employing flexibility in sequence, investigating local health demands and diversifying teaching aids

19. The BEST approach for the health teacher to use in an effort to enhance pupil participation and the quality of discussion is to 19._____

   A. allow volunteers to carry the discussion
   B. restrict the slow or shy pupil who may stall the discussion
   C. discourage the evaluation of student responses
   D. provide an answer himself rather than continually rephrase a question

20. All of the following are examples of behavioral objectives EXCEPT: 20._____

   A. "The student can list six links of the infectious disease process."
   B. "Under supervision, the student can safely apply a triangular bandage."

C. "The student chooses food in the cafeteria that comprises a well balanced diet."

D. "The student knows that communicable diseases are caused by microorganisms."

21. An auto-instructional approach to teaching relying on the psychological principles of reinforcement and associative learning is called   21.____

    A. programmed instruction   B. problem solving

    C. socio-dramitization   D. role playing

22. If a student's answer to a key question posed by the teacher is correct but ungrammatically expressed, of the following, it is WISEST for the teacher to   22.____

    A. interrupt the pupil's answer in order to correct the error

    B. ignore the error since the content of the answer is more important

    C. accept it and have the answer rephrased by another student

    D. ask the class what was wrong with the answer

23. In the use of a blackboard, all of the following are desirable practices EXCEPT the one in which the teacher   23.____

    A. provides sketches large enough so that they are visible to all pupils in the room

    B. places complex drawings on the blackboard in advance of the lesson to aid in pupils' understanding

    C. keeps all information on the blackboard to assit in the final summarization of the lesson

    D. stands to one side as he sketches a diagram or writes information

24. Of the following, the MOST desirable use of questioning during a lesson is the one which   24.____

    A. provides discovery of pupils' inadequate preparation of the lesson

    B. allows for the learning of the answers the teacher considers important enough to be remembered

    C. checks on pupil inattention during the development of the lesson

    D. focuses pupil attention on important aspects of the topic

25. During a lesson in health instruction, it is LEAST advisable to use audio-visual material   25.____

    A. when a new unit of work is being introduced

    B. during the body of the lesson in which these materials are the basis for the lesson

    C. as a means of summarizing the lesson

    D. as the means of encouraging spontaneous oral student reactions

26. Note-taking by pupils in a health lesson should be   26.____

    A. eliminated, since it detracts from the pupil's ability to listen attentively

    B. limited to the recording of the essentials presented during the lesson

    C. used by the teacher as a means of measuring the extent to which a pupil uses his notebook

    D. concerned with the copying of all notes from the blackboard which were presented during the lesson

27. In order to determine if a test question has the ability to discriminate between better and poorer students, the teacher should   27.____

    A. compare the results of the better students
    B. compare the results of the poorer students
    C. perform an item analysis
    D. perform a validity and reliability analysis

28. The BEST method of appraising the health understandings of students with language difficulties is the use of _____ tests.   28.____

    A. essay   B. oral
    C. objective   D. standardized achievement

29. If a teacher wanted to elicit from students spontaneous responses regarding any topic, the method she would have the MOST success with is called   29.____

    A. role playing   B. problem solving
    C. brainstorming   D. self appraisal

30. The MAIN purpose of a pivotal question is to   30.____

    A. direct thought from one aspect of a topic to another aspect of the same topic
    B. have students recall facts related to the topic being discussed
    C. drill students in specific knowledge previously learned
    D. encourage students to come up with a variety of answers

31. In providing for individual differences, of the following, the MOST advisable plan for the health teacher to adopt is to   31.____

    A. allow each child in the class complete freedom of choice in pursuing his projects
    B. have each student apprised of his specific weakness and to work toward correcting it
    C. arrange the students into small groups and plan his work so that the needs of each group are provided for
    D. provide short, frequent tests to determine variations in individual differences and to provide drill to reduce the variations

32. In dealing with slow learners in a heterogenous class, the teacher of health should   32.____

    A. exempt them from any special reports
    B. spread them throughout the classroom
    C. call upon them only if they volunteer
    D. require them to do the exact same homework assignments as others in the class

33. The MOST effective approach for a teacher to use in an alcohol education unit is to   33.____

    A. stress the evils of alcoholism
    B. emphasize the importance of the freedom of the individual to make responsible choices
    C. present facts about alcohol to the students
    D. use the scare approach to discourage students from using alcohol

34. In developing a program of treatment of the alcoholic, the LEAST important consideration is

    A. hospitalization until completion of the treatment
    B. detoxification
    C. physical rehabilitation including nutritional assistance
    D. maintenance of abstinence

35. One of the EARLIEST effects of alcohol on the body is

    A. reduced heart action
    B. loss of equilibrium
    C. decrease in judgment and self-control
    D. blurred and double vision

KEY (CORRECT ANSWERS)

1. A	16. D		
2. D	17. C		
3. A	18. D		
4. A	19. A		
5. D	20. D		
6. A	21. A		
7. D	22. B		
8. C	23. D		
9. D	24. D		
10. A	25. D		
11. C	26. B		
12. C	27. D		
13. A	28. B		
14. A	29. C		
15. C	30. A		

31. A
32. C
33. B
34. A
35. C

EXAMINATION SECTION
TEST 1

DIRECTIONS: Each question or incomplete statement is followed by several suggested answers or completions. Select the one that *BEST* answers the question or completes the statement. *PRINT THE LETTER OF THE CORRECT ANSWER IN THE SPACE AT THE RIGHT.*

1. As a result of an investigation of the fluoridation of public water supplies in the United States, scientists have reached all of the following conclusions *EXCEPT:*   1.____

    A. The fluoridation of water supplies will without doubt materially reduce the rate of tooth decay,
    B. The continued consumption of water containing as much as one part per million of fluorine is harmful.
    C. There is no evidence of any difference in the biological effect of artificially fluoridated water and that of naturally fluoridated water.
    D. No evidence exists of harm to the health from consumption of fluorides at recommended levels.

2. The American Dental Association endorses the statement that: 2.____

    A. Anti-enzyme toothpastes will prevent dental decay.
    B. Chlorophyl brands of tooth paste prevent diseases of the gums.
    C. The toothbrush, if properly used, is more effective than any particular substance in a toothpaste for preventing tooth decay.
    D. Ammoniated dentifrices reduce dental decay.

3. The "case conference" is *EAST* effective when   3.____

    A. teachers pool information concerning a student
    B. teachers verify observations of a student by comparing their findings
    C. teachers are enabled to see the consistency or inconsistency of a student's behavior in different situations
    D. each teacher selects the phase of the problem which he or she will help the student to solve

4. In planning field trips, the health teacher should   4.____

    A. use them as a pleasant surprise for the class
    B. plan to visit every place that extends a welcome
    C. plan to visit those places or activities that are related to the class activities
    D. allow the students to select those places where they are sure to receive samples

5. Of the following procedures for determining the effectiveness of your health teaching, the *LEAST* effective is to   5.____

    A. test the student's health knowledge
    B. determine the student's health status and his attempts at remedial procedures
    C. note the student's everyday health behavior
    D. determine the student's success in strength tests in physical activities

6. Of the following reasons for field trips in connection with the teaching of health, the *BEST* is that

    A. students will have an opportunity to listen to a prepared talk
    B. generally, textbooks are not sufficiently up-to-date
    C. the teacher has a limited knowledge of the subject
    D. students can see community activities in operation

7. In using a moving picture in a health lesson, it is *LEAST* advisable for the teacher to   7.____

    A. review the picture before showing it to the class
    B. draw up questions based on the film before it is presented to the class
    C. have certain parts of the film seen a second time by the students
    D. make running comments by way of explanation as the film progresses

8. To better understand behavior problems, the nurse-teacher should *FIRST*   8.____

    A. have a personal interview with the student
    B. observe the student in other classes
    C. examine the cumulative records of the student
    D. test the student

9. Superior performers in sports should be   9.____

    A. excused from the required physical education activities and be assigned to school service
    B. used as student assistants when their special skills are being taught
    C. given assignments as class secretaries or monitors
    D. assigned as assistant teachers to correct the errors of the students throughout the period

10. The only function *NOT* served by the student-leader in a health program is to   10.____

    A. act as a demonstrator during the teacher's verbal explanation
    B. inspire confidence in the performer
    C. help students experiment with new procedures the teacher hasn't had the time to teach to the entire group
    D. stand or kneel at the proper place so as to give instant help in an emergency

11. Of the following methods, the *one* that is *MOST* desirable for reducing teacher verbaliza-   11.____
tion is to

    A. allot more time for free choice of activity and for squad activity
    B. have different students conduct each phase of the lesson
    C. use skilled students to perform demonstrations and call for a critical analysis by the class
    D. post on the bulletin board pictures and other visual aids of the skills to be learned

12. Regarding the extent of the use of motivation in a health lesson, the *MOST* valid of the   12.____
following statements is:

    A. Every large phase of the lesson should be motivated, and medial motivations should be introduced where needed.
    B. A motivation is used to get the class started well.

C. The lesson should be motiviated when the class appears uninterested.

D. Motivation should be employed when the teaching of new skills is introduced.

13. During the teaching of a new skill, the teacher-nurse, while on the platform, should *avoid*   13.____

    A. facing the class and demonstrating the skill using the right arm and leg as the class performs with the left arm and leg

    B. combining a description and a demonstration of the skill

    C. using a pupil as a model for a demonstration of the skill

    D. standing with her back to the class as she demonstrates the skill for right-handed students and left-handed students

14. When teaching a health skill in mass formation, the teacher-nurse should be concerned   14.____
with all of the following *EXCEPT*

    A. correct individual performance

    B. a uniform start and halt

    C. sufficient repetition to insure learning

    D. motivating the skill

15. Of the following procedures for organizing group activities, the *MOST* desirable one for   15.____
the teacher to use is to

    A. have the class seated in front of the platform and then to demonstrate and fully describe the group activities

    B. send the groups to their activity areas and then instruct each group individually

    C. have the groups sit at their activity areas, and then teach the activities as you stand in the center of the room

    D. have the class seated in groups in front of the platform, give the groups just enough information to start their activities, and then visit each group in order to give additional information and to make corrections

16. The first center for premature infants was established at   16.____

    A. Bellevue Hospital

    B. Lincoln Hospital

    C. Kings County Hospital

    D. Babies' Hospital, Columbia Presbyterian Medical Center

17. When young children are very happy, they   17.____

    A. smile quietly

    B. laugh quietly

    C. play quietly

    D. roar, clap hands, jump up and down

18. The young child may be expected to acquire   18.____

    A. no skills   B. few skills

    C. the cruder skills   D. the finer skills

19. Young children like to hear a story told

    A. only once
    B. in a new form
    C. slightly changed
    D. daily, exactly as it was told before

20. The National Safety Council recommends the reporting of accidents which interrupt nor-
    mal activity *beyond*   20.__

    A. 24 hours   B. 72 hours   C. 48 hours   D. 36 hours

21. Of the following, the *MOST* frequent cause of death between ages of 15-34 is   21.__

    A. tuberculosis   B. accidents
    C. heart trouble   D. cancer

22. Children with tinea capitas may remain in school *BECAUSE*   22.__

    A. the disease is self-limiting
    B. the duration of the disease is short
    C. of school health services
    D. the classroom environment helps in its abatement

23. Diabetics are predisposed to   23.__

    A. tuberculosis   B. high blood pressure
    C. benign tumors   D. glaucoma

24. Learning occurs when   24.__

    A. the child's responses are adequate
    B. when a solution to the situation is obvious
    C. when the adult solves the problems
    D. none of the above

25. Since a child's skin is thinner than an adult's, therefore he feels pain   25.__

    A. *more* keenly
    B. *less* keenly
    C. to the same *degree* as the adult
    D. *much less* keenly

KEY (CORRECT ANSWERS)

1.	B	11.	C
2.	C	12.	A
3.	D	13.	D
4.	C	14.	B
5.	D	15.	D
6.	D	16.	D
7.	D	17.	D
8.	C	18.	C
9.	B	19.	D
10.	C	20.	A

21.	A
22.	A
23.	A
24.	A
25.	A

———

TEST 2

DIRECTIONS: Each question or incomplete statement is followed by several suggested answers or completions. Select the one that *BEST* answers the question or completes the statement. *PRINT THE LETTER OF THE CORRECT ANSWER IN THE SPACE AT THE RIGHT.*

1. The *first* emotions to become differentiated may be described as   1.___
   - A. anger and fear
   - B. anger and distress
   - C. fear and delight
   - D. delight and distress

2. A study of geriatrics shows a dietary need for   2.___
   - A. desserts   B. cereals   C. meat   D. liquids

3. A voluntary agency which has pioneered in gerontology is the   3.___
   - A. Young Men's Christian Association
   - B. Salvation Army
   - C. Union Health Center
   - D. Community Service Society

4. First priority for transportation during a nuclear catastrophe includes   4.___
   - A. third-degree burns exceeding 80% body surface
   - B. moderately severe burns up to 2% body surface
   - C. deep burns in individuals over 70
   - D. second-degree burns up to 70% body surface

5. Louis Pasteur is known for his work on   5.___
   - A. tuberculosis
   - B. smallpox
   - C. puerperal fever
   - D. rabies prevention

6. PUBLIC HEALTH REPORTS is published by the   6.___
   - A. United States Public Health Service
   - B. American Public Health Assocation
   - C. State Department of Health
   - D. City Department of Health

7. The form of play used *MOST* frequently by very young children is   7.___
   - A. construction play
   - B. dramatic play
   - C. parallel play
   - D. group play

8. If a school nurse were to give aspirin to a student, it would be   8.___
   - A. malpractice
   - B. in accord with the policy in most schools
   - C. practicing a profession for which she has no license
   - D. all right, if the principal approves

9. Prepayment medical plans have increased the need for   9.___
   - A. medical specialists
   - B. masseurs
   - C. family practitioners
   - D. chiropractors

10. The behavior pattern considered to be deviate by clinicians is   10.____

    A. infractions of the moral code
    B. generosity
    C. recessive personality
    D. resistance to authority

11. Typhoid fever is less prevalent *CHIEFLY* because of   11.____

    A. early detection   B. use of antibiotics
    C. control measures   D. fewer carriers

12. Generally, isolation must be provided for contacts to   12.____

    A. poliomyelitis only
    B. meningitis only
    C. neither poliomyelitis nor meningitis
    D. both diseases

13. Of the following, the *BEST* procedure to carry out in a tuberculosis detection and control   13.____
program in high schools would be to have

    A. chest x-rays of all teachers
    B. tuberculin tests on all teachers and students
    C. chest x-rays of all teachers and tuberculin tests on all students
    D. tuberculin tests on all teachers and chest x-rays of all students

14. In order to assist effectively in the prevention of deformity in her patient, the nurse must   14.____
know that muscle tone is *BEST* retained by

    A. "muscle setting"
    B. passive motion
    C. active motion
    D. active motion with muscles on the stretch

15. Despite reprimands, a student frequently disrupts your health activities class to the point   15.____
of physically endangering others in the class.
Of the following, the *MOST* effective solution to the problem would be to

    A. work with him in dual combatives
    B. assign him to work in a free area of the room away from the other students
    C. give him a solemn warning that you will not tolerate his actions another time
    D. have him taken out of the class for further administrative action

16. A secondary school program of physical education should provide all of the following   16.____
EXCEPT:

    A. The acquiring of sufficient skills to enable the student to get out of the "dub" class
       in a reasonable variety of activities
    B. With the more complicated sports, an emphasis on the beginning complex skills in
       the junior high school and an emphasis on the advanced skills in the senior high
       school

C. An opportunity through extra class programs for those students interested in per-fecting their skills

D. A program which offers primarily the four major sports in the country; namely, bas-ketball, softball, volleyball, and bowling, so that students will be well-grounded for their post-school lives

17. All of the following associations are *correct EXCEPT:*   17.___

A. Trudeau - leukemia   B. Holmgren - vision
C. Enders - poliomyelitis   D. Bancroft - posture

18. The program of our President's Council on Youth Fitness calls for all of the following mea-   18.___
sures *EXCEPT* a

A. minimum of 15 minutes a day of vigorous activity for all
B. wide variety of intramural sports outside of school hours for all children
C. regular instructional program in health and safety education for all grades
D. testing program to spot the physically below-par children so that they can be sepa-rated from those who regularly get developmental exercises

19. Of the following, the *CORRECT* statement is: 19.___

A. All people with rosy complexions are healthy.
B. Any food that does not smell or taste spoiled is safe to eat.
C. All children with heart murmurs will surely have heart trouble later on in life.
D. Most persons who look thin and underweight are not necessarily in poor health.

20. Of the following publications, the one of *LEAST* value to the health counselor is: 20.___

A. Directory of Social Agencies
B. Guide for Health Counselors
C. Manual of Procedures for School Medical Services
D. Directory of Private and Public Hospitals

21. Totaling the scores made in a physical fitness test and dividing that sum by the number   21.___
of individuals will give the _____ for the group.

A. mode   B. median
C. mean   D. standard deviation

22. Of the following, it is *CORRECT* to state that the intelligence quotient   22.___

A. is a permanent recording of the individual's characteristics
B. indicates the present level of a child's intellectual attainment
C. shows the individual's true intellectual capacity
D. will remain the same when different intelligence tests are employed

23. In an attempt to keep disciplinary problems in a health class to a minimum, all of the fol-   23.___
lowing are recommended for teacher action *EXCEPT* to

A. exercise self-discipline so that a student does not feel that the teacher is emotion-ally involved in his misbehavior
B. show authority from the outset so that correct behavior is established at the start

C. divide your time and attention equally, so far as possible, among all members of the class
D. refrain from sarcasm and personal remarks in addressing the class

24. In general, the teacher's verbal explanation should   24.____

   A. include the use of adolescent slang, in order to be understood
   B. begin with something the students already know
   C. be more lengthy for the beginner than for the advanced participant
   D. tell "how" the activity is to be done, rather than "why"

25. Of the following, the *LEAST* advisable procedure during the showing of a film in a health   25.____
lesson is the one in which the

   A. film is halted at the midway mark in order to question students on the content of the film shown
   B. students take notes during the showing of the film
   C. teacher keeps a list of new terms as they appear during the presentation of the film
   D. students" seats are rearranged in order to provide a clear view of the screen

-----

KEY (CORRECT ANSWERS)

1.	D	11.	D
2.	C	12.	C
3.	D	13.	C
4.	D	14.	C
5.	D	15.	D
6.	A	16.	D
7.	C	17.	A
8.	C	18.	D
9.	C	19.	D
10.	C	20.	C

21.	C
22.	B
23.	B
24.	B
25.	B

CPSIA information can be obtained
at www.ICGtesting.com
Printed in the USA
LVHW060209140919
631097LV00027B/390/P

9 781731 858009